WHAT OTHERS ARE SAYING A

G000123259

My hope is that this will become a sought-aft~
through by anyone who is serious about living a lifestyle that r~~~
of God.

If you are feeling left out, misunderstood, isolated, or have questions about God's ability to release the fullness of His life into your life, then this book is for you. Ken Symington speaks from his heart, gives vivid illustrations, and answers some of the most pressing questions that many of us wrestle with, or silently ask. I often say at our ministry conferences that corporate transformation always begins with the individual, and that you cannot with integrity expect your church, your business, your community, and even your city to go further than you yourself have gone.

So be prepared! *The Great Adventure* has the ability to change your life! By that I mean you cannot simply read this book, see scripture and live out one's Christian life in the same way ever again. Putting it another way, this book is a blueprint for living one's life *in* Christ and *for* Christ in a manner that will shift the reader from a life of mediocrity to one that experiences and reflects the power and relevance of the Kingdom of God. If the message in this book is applied correctly, expect to receive vision – insight – direction – even correction – along with a fresh understanding of Godly counsel and discipline. Above all, the message in this book releases new hope and passion for anyone seeking more in their Christian journey, since what may simply have been "learned behavior" up until this moment, will suddenly become an adventure!

Rev. Dr. Alistair Petrie
Author and Executive Director, Partnership Ministries, Canada
www.partnershipministries.org

It is a rare occurrence to find a book that so clearly and passionately encapsulates the Kingdom of Jesus Christ and how to live wholeheartedly in His Kingdom today. This book exposes and addresses the many things that are eroding and undermining the effectiveness of believers today and steadily guides us back to the plumb line of biblical truth. At the same time, it reaches out and rekindles within us that God given desire for "more". You will not fail to be both challenged and inspired as you read this book and I pray that it will stir you to press on and take hold of all that Jesus died to give you. Ken's first book, *Loved Like Never Before*, is our number one bestseller at Ellel Pierrepont and I believe this book will even outstrip that.

Jill Southern-Jones
Centre Director - Ellel Pierrepont, UK
www.ellelministries.org/uk/about/ellel-pierrepont

Someone once said that becoming a Christian is free, but becoming a follower of Jesus is costly!! How true that is, but how true it is that very few Christians have ever really been taught this cost or have even been helped to understand this truth. The results of this kind of a free and easy Christian life are not hard to see, a form of godliness but without any real impacting difference being made on the world that our Father God so loved. If we are going to make a difference in our world we are going to have to be different.

A true follower of Jesus will be different, not the freaky kind we see too often today, but the naturally supernatural kind, who carry the presence and power of Christ in them to be His difference makers. Extraordinary Christians who know their God and do great exploits for Him

Everywhere Jesus Christ went he made an impact and left His difference behind. In the making of such a follower of Jesus, there are many ingredients needed to make the real thing and keep the main thing the main thing! Like a great cake its very essence is dependant upon the ingredients that are put into it and it's greatness is proved in the power of its taste. This book by Ken Symington provides the would be follower of Jesus Christ not only with the right ingredients, but also with the right mix and balanced understanding that will help them become the real thing

As a pastor who wants to see his flock flourish, the greatest asset of Ken Symington to the church is not just his tremendous knowledge of the things of God... many people have that, but it is his understanding of that knowledge that, for me, really distinguishes this book from all the rest. This is what has given him the ability to get the mix and balance right. Firstly it will prevent Gods people being destroyed by a lack of knowledge and live an ordinary-kind of life; secondly it will help the true follower of Jesus become His difference in the world, living a life of adventure as they follow Jesus.

If you want to live an ordinary Christian life then this book isn't for you. But if you want to go on a great adventure and lead to an extraordinary life in the power of the Holy Spirit, this book by Ken Symington is a must!

Jeff Wright
Lead Pastor, Green pastures - the people's church, Northern Ireland

When I'm looking at the car and motorcycle sales web sites sometimes I see an advertisement that says "No tire-kickers". What this is saying is that the seller doesn't want to waste his time showing the car to people who only want to have a look, but aren't really serious about wanting to buy.

From my experience in the body of Christ I sense that there are many Christians who are "tire-kickers" when it comes to following Jesus Christ. Being a disciple is not a hobby, one that fits in alongside other interests in a person's life.

I love the way Ken challenges us to walk the walk. His teaching, his writing and the way he lives stirs me to be completely surrendered to Christ, my Savior and Lord.

This book should carry a warning sticker - "Not for Tire-kickers".

Rev Paul Watson
Regional Director, Australia-Pacific, Ellel Ministries

The call to follow Jesus is a combination of invitation and challenge. Ken Symington, in his new book *The Great Adventure* seeks to provide a clear framework of teaching that teases out what that invitation and challenge looks like if we really want to follow Jesus. With his conversational style and easily accessible language, he poses some basic questions which lie at the heart of discipleship and in doing so 'laces' his book with Scripture, stories and personal reflection on his own journey so far.

By writing this book Ken adds his voice to a growing number of voices who recognise that the greatest need of the 21st century church in the West is for disciples - those who will really follow Jesus in the 'nitty gritty' of everyday life.

The ultimate challenge of this book is a call for all apprentices (disciples) of Jesus, in the power of the Holy Spirit, 'to do' the truth as we follow the one 'who is' the truth. Ken urges us to embrace this challenge and in doing so to enter into 'The Great Adventure'.

Rev. Francis Rutledge
Christ Church Primacy, Northern Ireland

To listen to Ken Symington teaching is not like listening to anyone else. He is down-to-earth, clear, means what he says and says what he means. His book, *The Great Adventure*, has the same character. It has an intriguing second title line: "The challenge of really following Jesus". The word "really" stands out, makes this book different from so many others on the same subject. It tells me that Ken means business. It is a book that challenges you in many ways, but that never leaves any doubt that you can be that real follower. It is simply a handbook for those who want to live the adventure that is called a Christian life in a non-Christian world.

Ken is the best guide to such a life that I can imagine. He is not luke-warm. He believes in the Word of God, and he bases everything he says on that reality. He also lives it out, and that gives him an enormous amount of experience to share with the reader: "It is written, I have tried it, and it works!"

This is not a book for the book-shelf, it is for repeated reading and daily digesting for those who are honest about their desire to be real with God. It is a book that will greatly help you get going in your great adventure, really following Jesus.

I cannot strongly enough recommend this book. It is a book that shows the way from being an average Christian to being totally, radically and eternally committed to following Jesus. Whoever you are, wherever you live, and whatever the cost, if you are not ready for that, read this book at your own peril!

Goran Anderson

Retired Director, Ellel Sweden; former missionary to Japan (18 years)

The Great Adventure

The challenge of *really* following Jesus

by

Ken Symington

CHI-Books
PO Box 6462
Upper Mt Gravatt, Brisbane
QLD 4122, Australia

www.chibooks.org
publisher@chibooks.org

The Great Adventure
The challenge of really following Jesus

Print edition ISBN: 978-0-9875608-4-1
eBook edition ISBN: 978-0-9875608-5-8

Printed in Australia, United Kingdom and the United States of America.

Distributed globally via a range of internet distribution outlets like: Ingram Book Group, Amazon.com and BookDepository.com. Distributed in the USA via Spring Arbor - Christian Alliance nationwide, Barnes & Nobel and others. Distributed in the UK and Europe through distribution outlets like Wesley Owen and Koorong UK. Also available through Chapters in Canada and Koorong in Australia.

Global eBook distribution available through outlets like the Amazon Kindle store, Apple iBookstore, Barnes & Nobel Nook, Sony eReader and others.

Editorial assistance: Anne Hamilton

Cover design: Dave Stone

Layout: Jonathan Gould

CONTENTS

Thanks and appreciation

Thank you Jesus for the gift of my wonderful wife, Linda.

For the gift of four wonderful children, Scott, Joanne, Stephen and David.

For the gift of four wonderful grandchildren, Matthew, Alexander, Anna and Will.

For two wonderful sisters, Shireen and Jill.

And for the amazing team of men and women who continue to play such a major role in the ministry you have entrusted to me.

Foreword

You hold in your hands a brilliant discipleship tool in Ken Symington's **THE GREAT ADVENTURE**—*the challenge of really following Jesus*. But before I speak about the book, let me tell you about the man.

When I first met Ken Symington quite a few years ago he was teaching at a conference I attended in the UK. It was around the time I had become tired of my mediocre Christianity and was searching for something deeper than I'd experienced up to that point in my life. His challenging teaching that weekend sparked something within me. I was no longer content with mediocrity.

Today Ken is a personal friend and he has been a significant mentor. I love his eye for great landscape photography and his passion for outdoor pursuits. He happens to be a very handy fisherman too! I also really appreciate the fact he is an extremely funny guy! However, if I was asked to summarize Ken, I would say he is one of the few men I know who've learned to live an undivided life for Christ, one who serves God wholeheartedly. Ken actually models what that kind of life looks like. And he does it powerfully.

When I watch Ken in his marriage to Linda, I am reminded that Jesus is returning for His Bride. When I watch Ken relate tenderly to his children, or grand-children… I see my Heavenly Father at work. When Ken teaches, the conviction of Holy Spirit is always present to empower and bring life transformation to those he impacts.

Ken is a man of deep integrity. Where weaker men would adopt a lie to save themselves… Ken will choose the truth—regardless of its consequences!—because he trusts that the God of all Truth will stand by him. Ken rightly states in this book: *'mature sons and daughters are different. Very different. The world has little hold on them.'* Ken's life indeed demonstrates that to me.

Charles Spurgeon is quoted in this book with this statement: *'When my classroom is darkest, I see best.'* That sentence epitomizes some hallmarks of

Ken's own journey. It recognizes the trials, difficulties and dark days that have forged his character to date.

He has suffered under incredibly difficult life circumstances at times, yet he has never allowed such events to embitter him. Instead, in each difficult situation he chose to trust his Heavenly Father through those trials. In so doing, I have noticed on the other side of each test, the Lord released a new earned authority over Ken that could not have been gained any other way. Ken's story reminds us that God's character is rarely developed in us during the easier, less traumatic periods of life. This book soberly reminds us it is usually during the darker struggles of life that God hones us in a deeper way.

Drawing from the great C.S. Lewis, I can find no better words to describe Ken Symington's response in the midst of extreme duress than to paraphrase words taken from, letter number eight, *The Screwtape Letters*:

"The cause of evil is never more in danger then when someone, no longer desiring but still intending to do the Father's will, looks around upon a universe from which every trace of God seems to have vanished and they ask why they have been forsaken... yet they still obey!"

I don't know about you... but I want to be led by men like that! Men who under enormous pressure, facing illness, tragedy and disaster still choose to trust and obey God! This is the life model Ken Symington has witnessed to me. And for me, that is important. Because now that I know the man and have seen his character withstand the tests and pressure that has come upon him on numerous occasions... I now know I can trust his message.

The Apostle Paul in the New Testament states we do not have many fathers in the faith. Ken Symington, thankfully, is indeed a 'father' that the Body of Christ desperately needs in order to show us how we should be living in the hour we find ourselves in. His writings in this book sound a warning and offer a significant challenge to us.

The Church in many ways and in too many places has fallen asleep and is 'sailing' dangerously close to 'inshore reefs and rocks'. Ken is in effect sounding the alarm, much like A.W. Tozer sounded the alarm to his generation. Ken's book, *The Great Adventure—the challenge of really following Jesus*, I believe carries a crucial prophetic message for this generation! This book offers a sure path, an ancient path, one that unveils kingdom keys essential for our journey into wholeness and maturity.

There is no 'sugar-coating' to be found here... this is a serious book on discipleship! In Ken's own words: *'The Church is wonderfully awash with believers, but in truth, very few disciples.'* Ken wants to see the fragrance of Christ upon every disciple's life. He desires to see that aroma impact as many as possible. However, Ken recognizes that his message will not be for every believer, but only those who are tired of mediocrity and prepared to pay the price to be a true disciple of Jesus Christ.

What you have in your hand right now is an invitation to an amazing adventurous life in Christ. If you are bored with mediocre Christianity as I was... then turn the page...

Paul Ryan

Centre Director, Ellel Ministries, "Gilbulla"
Sydney, Australia

Prelude

I did feel guilty and rightly so! I had blatantly told lies to a group of lovely Christian people and my conscience was working overtime within me.

I was having lunch with workmates and recounting the difficulty I found myself in. Several weeks earlier I had messed up big time in the annual all–Ireland triathlon in County Sligo (a 1 mile sea swim, 56 mile cycle and 13 mile run). I was still mad at myself for the schoolboy error I'd committed. After 10 years of daily training and continual competing at a senior level, I had finally made the 'elite' group of triathletes in Ireland, being rated 28th out of the 300 athletes taking part. So I was targeting a 'Top 20' placing. I was also determined to come second in the veterans' age group (40+) after placing third in the previous two years.

I knew the event would take between three and four hours to complete. I knew, *we all knew*, you needed a good breakfast as fuel for the day, plus snacks in pockets and bike pouches to consume along the way. On the morning of the race I felt so strong, so fit, so ready to race I told my wife I would skip breakfast so I could perform faster with nothing to digest. I would take no snacks.

And yes, I'm sure you can guess what happened. With no big breakfast to digest I had a really good swim, then a great bike leg, and in the run was well on my way to my best–ever performance when three miles from the finish line I hit 'the wall'. I pleaded with the crowd to give, or get me a chocolate bar or banana. Nothing was forthcoming. Runners I had passed earlier were now passing me. It was heartbreaking.

With only one mile left I was walking. Then I sat down on the road, before walking again and finally collapsing over the finish line. I was totally, completely, exhausted.

Even with this disaster I still finished 32nd. I could only imagine how close to the top I might have finished had I eaten properly. I was *so* angry with myself. I could talk about little else over the following week and I drove everyone potty!

However, the Northern Ireland Championships were coming up in a few weeks time—in which I had finished 9th overall in the previous two years— so I determined that I would train harder than ever to see if I could, in some way, make up for my earlier stupidity. But how could I train harder? I already trained at lunch times and evenings. (Yes, my poor family!)

Then God's trap began to close. We had belonged to the local Methodist church for some ten years. Several evenings after we returned from the All Ireland event, the minister phoned Linda to ask if we would like to come to the annual week–long Methodist Holiday Camp at Castlewellan Country Park. He explained there was still one caravan available. Linda put her hand over the phone and asked me if I wanted to go. My immediate reaction was a most certain 'no thanks'.

But then, inspiration! There was a lake at Castlewellan Country Park, a running track around it, and excellent cycling roads in the area. I could get a week off work and take the family there. They could go to the 'churchy' bits at the big tent in the mornings while I would go training instead. That would perhaps give me the extra strength and fitness I needed for the upcoming championship. Pleased with the prospect, I asked Linda to accept his kind invitation.

However it didn't work out as smoothly as I'd hoped. The evening we arrived lots of people made a point of warmly welcoming us. I quickly realized I would be expected to attend the 'churchy' bits every morning and could not just skip off on my swim, cycle and run training schedule.

So what did I do? I lied to them. I told them that, much as I would love to go the tent meetings every morning, I had to go to work every morning. However my wife and children would be there all right. And so it worked.

The first morning when everyone was in the tent, I was speeding around the roads on my ultra–light racing bike. Feeling horribly guilty. So horribly guilty, I decided I would actually go to work the next day. I would miss the tent meeting and so would not technically be telling a lie. It had all gone disastrously wrong.

I shared this sad tale with my colleagues over lunch. They were sympathetic. (I was their boss, so it was the smart attitude to take!) Finally I made my decision. I didn't want to keep making a round trip of nearly 50 miles every morning just to get out of the tent meetings with a semi–clean conscience. So I decided to man–up and just go to the meetings with my family.

It was interesting—full of people raising their arms in the air, clapping and sometimes dancing. Well, sort of dancing. 'We' didn't do silly things like that at 'our church'. But at least it was bearable. A little strange at first, but bearable. The people were genuine and lovely.

On the last morning the evangelist was describing the apostle Paul's life in some detail. Paul (then called Saul) had been a great achiever and was highly thought of by his peers. He described himself this way,

> *... circumcised on the eighth day, of the people of Israel, of the tribe of Benjamin, a Hebrew of Hebrews; in regard to the law, a Pharisee; as for zeal, persecuting the church; as for righteousness based on the law, faultless.* Philippians 3:5–6

And yet, from a Roman prison[1] he wrote to the church in Philippi telling them he counted all of this as garbage for the beauty of knowing Christ. I was uncomfortable. I began to have a sneaky feeling that, despite my company Porsche, my wife's company Volvo estate, my business awards and my sporting achievements I was possibly the poorest man there. These people had something priceless within them I definitely did not have, and I was beginning to understand what, or whom, that was. I was beginning to understand what Paul was saying, and I was becoming more and more uncomfortable with this growing understanding.

A lady behind me kept calling out "praise the Lord!" and I wanted to turn round and ask her to be quiet. But of course I didn't. Still I thought about it. Then I wanted to get up and leave, but I knew I wouldn't. I was too polite. The evangelist said that, if anyone wanted to give their life to Jesus, they should come and sit in one of the empty seats in the front row. "Why is he saying that?" I thought. "Doesn't he know we all go to church?"

Then he said that anyone who came forward should not sit on the seats, but kneel on the grass in front of the stage. "Now he's lost the plot," I thought.

"Come now," he said. I jumped to my feet, went forward and knelt. And there beside me was my wife.

Some fifteen years later I made a pilgrimage. I went down to Castlewellan Country Park on my own. I worked out where the tent would have been pitched, where the stage would have been and then where it was I would have knelt. And I tearfully thanked God for luring me to that blessed spot on August 11th 1989.

INTRODUCTION

Loved one.

This book will hopefully be the end of Christianity–lite[2] in your life.

Let me explain what I mean.

You're a Christian. A believer. Soundly saved by the grace of God.

You know you are loved by God.[3] You attend church. Perhaps a mid–week home group or Bible class.

You read your Bible daily (most days) and you pray.

And, more or less, that's it.

You're aware your spiritual life has become somewhat dry and predictable, yet you know following Jesus should be the greatest adventure of your life. And at times, deeply challenging. You know there has to be more. You *hunger* for more.

This book is for those who take, or want to take, their walk with Jesus seriously.

No more nominal Christianity. No more compromise. No more luke–warmness.

What counts in the end is a life that counts.

And what counts is our heartfelt response to those two words from Jesus.

"Follow Me."[4]

ONE
Who is Boss?

This chapter underpins everything else that follows.

The quote *'Jesus is Lord'* is a well–known and much–used phrase in Christian circles but, truth be told, in today's culture it makes little impact on our Christianity.

If you live in the United Kingdom, the word 'Lord' usually means someone who, after a long and successful career in public service, arts and culture or business, has been invited to sit in The House of Lords to bring wise counsel to Parliament procedures. It can conjure up pictures of elderly dignitaries making long speeches to a partly–filled chamber. Some who are awake. Some who are perhaps not–so–awake.

The exclamation 'good lord!' has almost become akin to swearing.

The Greek word for 'Lord' in Greek is usually *Kurios** but occasionally the word *despotes*** (des–pot–ace) is used, which is the origin of the English word 'despot'. A despot is someone who rules a kingdom with absolute

---

*	He to whom a person or thing belongs, about which he has power of deciding; master, lord; the possessor and disposer of a thing; the owner; one who has control of the person, the master; in the state: the sovereign, prince, chief, the Roman emperor; is a title of honour expressive of respect and reverence, with which servants greet their master; this title is given to God, the Messiah.
**	Luke 2:29, Revelation 6:10

authority, including supremacy over life and death. In Bible times Kings, Pharaohs, Caesars and Emperors were despots.

Perhaps you see where this is going!

Jesus' title is not only 'Lord', but also 'Lord of Lords'. And 'King of Kings'. And this could easily be adapted to 'Caesar of Caesars', 'Pharaoh of Pharaohs' and 'Emperor of Emperors'.

I became a Christian in August 1989. Aged 42. I had been raised in a Christian home and said my prayers every night since the age of three.

I still remember my simple childhood prayer.

"My Father for another night, for quiet sleep and rest, for all the joy of morning light, Thy holy name be blessed. Amen."

I was sent to, and quite liked, Sunday school. I went to church most Sundays with my parents. Even though I stopped going to church in my teens—only returning in my early thirties—I still prayed every night. I always believed in Jesus and understood the work of the cross. When attending church 'religiously' every Sunday in my thirties, I tithed, took communion and hosted a cell group in our home every two weeks. Despite having secret sin, I usually prayed for up to an hour on my knees every night.

Yet—as I look back on those days—I realize with clarity that I was not a Christian. I was certainly a supporter of Christianity and 'a friend' of God, but not a Christian.

Some may choose to disagree. However I know the difference before and after the morning of August 11th, 1989.

Before that date I was the Lord of my own life. After that date Jesus was the Lord of my life. My very simple but heartfelt prayer to Him was this…

> "Lord Jesus, I have been doing things my way for forty–two years. If you can do anything with the rest of my life, it's yours—lock, stock and barrel"

And suddenly everything changed. Within hours I realized my heart was filled to overflowing with the love of Christ, which began to outpour to others. The Bible came alive. My desire was to serve Jesus all the days of my life. The miracle of the new birth!

In the early weeks after my conversion, it seemed every time I opened the Bible I was confronted with the truth about the 'Lordship' of Jesus. It tasted sweet to my spirit. It also seemed that, in every conversation, I ended up talking about the Lordship of Jesus.

However, as week after week went by and I continued to be confronted with the truth about the Lordship of Jesus, I began to think I was becoming obsessive. One sunny Sunday afternoon, as I sat in our back garden, again saturated with Lordship thoughts, I cried out to Jesus to free me from this 'obsession'.

That evening Linda and I set out to attend church. To get there—a journey of perhaps two miles—meant passing through three traffic roundabouts on the town's ring road. As I went to drive through the second roundabout I found myself turning right, rather than continuing straight. Not surprisingly, Linda asked me where I was going! Somewhat confused, I replied I didn't know. I circled around the roundabout with the intention of continuing straight across town.

But again it happened. As I began my third circle, I suddenly realized what was happening. A new church was opening that evening along the road on the right hand side of the roundabout. I knew then that, on this particular evening, the Holy Spirit was directing us to this new church, rather than to our regular one. Nervously we parked in the church car park and made our way to the front door. We went through

> When you come to the cross of Christ in repentance for your rebellion against God you are in effect surrendering this self–rule over your life.

into the large auditorium where, stretched across the top of the stage, in large bold letters, was the statement: *'Jesus Is Lord.'*

No escape!

But with that final divine sign–off, this season of obsessiveness came to an end. Job done. This foundational truth was now deeply embedded within me. Jesus is LORD. Jesus is *my* Lord.

In Genesis, we read of God giving mankind freedom—except for one thing. He would tell them what was good and what was evil.[5] We know what happened. And what is still happening. Adam chose to decide what was good and what was evil. He would determine for himself what was right and what was wrong. God's rule was out. Man's self–rule was in.[6]

The rest is horrible history.

When you come to the cross of Christ in repentance for your rebellion against God you are in effect surrendering this self–rule over your life. You step down as Lord and instead you enthrone Him as Lord.

> *That if you confess with your mouth, "**Jesus is Lord**," and believe in your heart that God raised Him from the dead, you will be saved.* Romans 10:9 [emphasis mine]

And remarkably, instead of a prisoner–of–war camp for surrendering rebels, there is a banqueting table spread out and a banner over it saying, 'Love'.[7]

You are home. Like the prodigal you are home. Willingly, joyfully and humbly returning to your rightful place under the rule of God the Father through Jesus. God's will becomes your will.

Remember these well known lines from the Lord's prayer?

> ***Your*** *kingdom come.* ***Your will*** *be done on earth as it is in heaven.* Matthew 6:10 [emphasis mine]

Just as an apple tree bears apples as its natural fruit, so obedience is, *or should be*, the natural fruit of our salvation because it reflects our redeemed heart.

Charles Haddon Spurgeon said, "We are not saved by obedience, for obedience is the result of salvation! We are saved by faith, because faith leads us to obey!"[8]

In submitting ourselves to God's absolute rule and reign in Christ we find freedom. *Real* freedom. As Robin Mark's song declared: "It's only in your will that I am free."[9] If God says it is right, then it is right. If He says it is wrong, then it is wrong. He's the Boss.

The idea is simple. We can say, "Yes Lord," or "No," but we can't say, "No Lord." That is a contradiction. We are no longer the people who, in the parable of Jesus, say, 'We don't want this man to be our king.'[10]

Here and in the following pages, it is important to grasp God's truth with *your heart*,[11] so that it *spiritually empowers you*, rather than just with your mind, otherwise submission can become a 'must do' duty rather than a life giving joy.

So, with this understanding, listen now to Jesus with the ears of your heart. What is He saying? What is He establishing?

> *"Not everyone who says to Me, 'Lord, Lord,' will enter the kingdom of heaven, but only he who **does the will of My Father** who is in heaven."* Matthew 7:21 [emphasis mine]

> *"Why do you call me, 'Lord, Lord,' and do not do what I say?"* Luke 6:46

> *He replied, "My mother and brothers are those who hear God's word and **put it into practice**."* Luke 8:21 [emphasis mine]

The apostle John ensured that the flock understood this very foundational truth by using—what was for him—strong language:

The man who says, 'I know Him,', but does not do what He says is a liar, and the truth is not in him. 1 John 2:4

The writer of Hebrews assumed that obedience went hand in hand with salvation:

...and, once made perfect, He became the source of eternal salvation for all who obey Him... Hebrews 5:9

Paul emphasized the absolute Lordship of Jesus:

...at the name of Jesus every knee should bow, in heaven and on earth and under the earth. Philippians 2:10

The wind and the waves obeyed Him.[12] The fish obeyed Him.[13] The demons obeyed Him.[14] If we don't obey Him, what does that make us?

Charles Haddon Spurgeon said, "If the professed convert distinctly and deliberately declares that he knows the Lord's will but does not mean to attend to it, you are not to pamper his presumption, but it is your duty to assure him that he is not saved."[15]

> Obedience, child–like obedience, means that I now sincerely desire to do His will in the workplace, in the home, in my social life and in church.

My willing submission to Jesus as my Lord was the event that changed my life forever, and began my journey. For many years prior to that date, I had known what God's Word said but it never, *ever*, entered my thinking I was actually supposed to do it! How many times over those years must I have prayed, "Forgive us our sins, for we also forgive everyone who sins against us,"[16] without it dawning on me that I was actually meant to forgive those who sinned against me! It could be likened to setting a hearty meal in front of a starving man and asking him if he believed this meal could save his life. He says, "Yes," but months later you find a skeleton sitting in front of the uneaten meal. Believing without doing is not true believing.[17]

The Apostle James wrote to the church (us):

> Do not merely listen to the word, and so deceive yourselves. **Do what it says**. James 1:22 [emphasis mine]

Obedience, child–like obedience,[18] means that I now sincerely desire to do His will in the workplace, in the home, in my social life and in church. Sadly never done perfectly—but always with a heart set to loving obedience and also to repentance when I get it wrong.[19]

On my computer at work (before I entered full–time ministry), where only I could see it, was a note asking, "Ken, what would Jesus do?" In daily decision times I could, with one glance, and without needing chapter and verse, know what was 'right' and what was 'wrong'. Then I had to choose whether to do it (submit) or not do it (rebel).[20]

As a husband I have to ask myself, "Am I genuinely trying to treat my wife the way Jesus treats us, the church, His bride?"[21] As a father I have to ask myself if I am reflecting the heart of God the Father to my children, and now my grandchildren.[22] As a church member, am I in Godly submission?[23] As a member of society, am I in respectful submission to the proper authorities?[24] As a child of God, a son of God, am I influenced by the world and its godless ways or does the Word of God influence me?[25] (But more on this in chapter three!)

John the beloved would not, could not, separate *love and obedience*.

> And this is love: that we walk in obedience to His commands. As you have heard from the beginning, His command is that you walk in love. 2 John 1:6

Religion tries to change you from the outside, while Jesus changes you from the inside.

Because of course, neither could Jesus:

"If you love Me, keep My commands." John 14:15

Here's the big idea. Religion tries to change you from the outside, while Jesus changes you from the inside. And to do this, He must be Lord. He does not force that position upon you. He stands and knocks.[26]

With this foundational block in place we can move on in our dramatic, life–changing journey.

Some probing questions:

- When did you yield your life to Jesus?

- Can you think of an occasion when the Lordship of Jesus overruled a decision or action you would otherwise have made?

- Is there an area where you are still Lord of your life?

TWO
The Sacrificial Lifestyle

I remember an advertising campaign designed to evoke support for the growing numbers of heavy lorries that were starting to dominate our roads. Lorries are rarely a problem on motorways but, along narrow roadways or when delivering, maneuvering or parking in city streets, they can definitely create problems. So, quite a task you might think for the advertising agency, but they nailed it with just one short sentence. "If you have it, it came by lorry." I tried to wriggle out of that broad sweeping statement but, by and large, it convinced me. I softened my frustration towards the mobile monsters and their crews.

Sacrifice is not a popular theme. In our humanity we are 'naturally' keener to focus on security and comfort than on sacrifice. But for the Christian who is hungry to move on with God, there is just no escaping this vital aspect of our relationship with Him. So here's the line. "Everything we have comes to us by sacrifice."

The word 'sacrifice' simply permeates Scripture. The word occurs around one hundred and fifty times. From the early chapters in Scripture it becomes clear that our relationship with God is established through sacrifice.

> *Then God said, "Take your son, your only son, whom you love—*
> *Isaac—and go to the region of Moriah. Sacrifice him there as a burnt*

> The Christian lifestyle was always meant to be a sacrificial lifestyle, because loving always involves sacrifice.

offering on a mountain I will show you." Genesis 22:2

"And when your children ask you, 'What does this ceremony mean to you?' then tell them, 'It is the Passover sacrifice to the Lord, who passed over the houses of the Israelites in Egypt and spared our homes when he struck down the Egyptians.'" Exodus 12:26–27

The seemingly endless and bloody Old Testament sacrifices from man's side towards God were but a shadow of the shockingly dramatic sacrifice that, at 'the right time'[27], would come from God's side towards man. Hanging on that cruel Roman cross, God's bloodied Son[28] became the once–and–for–all–time sacrificial Lamb.[29] From that excruciatingly painful, naked and lonely 'it is finished' moment[30] onwards, we would forever come to God through Jesus and, in addition, God's blessings would forever come to us through Jesus.[31] But you know that, don't you?

Here's where we are going with this. The Christian lifestyle was always meant to be a sacrificial lifestyle, because loving always involves sacrifice.[32] All precious Kingdom advances have come—and will continue to come—through personal sacrifice to one degree or another. Think of the cost to the apostles and the first disciples. To the martyrs. To the centuries of missionaries who have gone to the furthermost corners of the world. Think of the tireless Bible translators, the travelling evangelists and the itinerant teachers. Think of the Christian doctors who have chosen to forsake wealth at home in order to serve Jesus in third world countries. Think of pastors who sacrifice a normal family life to give almost permanent service to the flock entrusted to them. Think of the hours of practice that many devoted worship leaders put in week after week as well as the faithful church elders who visit the sick, the lonely and the bereaved. Think of those who labor week after week in prayer ministry and counseling. Or in relentless intercession on our behalf. Think of the overworked and usually poorly–paid church and ministry staff. Many of them unseen and unsung.

Not serving for personal gain or fame, but as a loving sacrifice to Jesus. Take away the sacrificial lifestyle and Christ's Kingdom will not advance as God intends it to advance.[33] Take away the sacrificial lifestyle and you are left with a lifeless church.[34]

Thus, when teachings are focused *only* on what Jesus has sacrificed in love for us, we can miss the important and spiritually empowering truth that Jesus calls us to live a sacrificial lifestyle in love for Him.[35] He modeled the sacrificial life and linked following Him with the sacrificial life.[36] The Old Testament is awash with the bodies of dead sacrifices[37] reverentially laid on the altar,[38] but the apostle Paul, writing to the community of Christians in Rome, urged them (and of course, us) to offer their bodies to God as a 'living' sacrifice.

> *Therefore, I urge you, brothers and sisters, in view of God's mercy, to offer your bodies as a living sacrifice, holy and pleasing to God—**this is your true and proper worship**.* Romans 12:1 [emphasis mine]

And of course he walked the talk. Just as Jesus was his example, so he wanted his life to be an example to others.[39] He has certainly influenced me in my walk with Jesus, and one day I will have the honor of meeting him in heaven and saying, "Thank you." Few of us will experience even a fraction of what serving Jesus cost Paul, but the principle is there. "Everything we have comes to us by sacrifice." I drew a simple lifeline of Paul's life starting with his conversion and ending with his death at Rome. Not in timeline order, but simply as a compacted sample of his sacrificial life.

He talked and debated with the Hellenistic Jews, but they tried to kill him.
Acts 9:29

To this very hour we go hungry and thirsty, we are in rags, we are brutally treated, we are homeless. We work hard with our own hands. When we are cursed, we bless; when we are persecuted, we endure it; when we are slandered, we answer kindly. We have become the scum of the earth, the garbage of the world - right up to this moment.
1 Cor 4: 11-13

The crowd joined in the attack against Paul and Silas, and the magistrates ordered them to be stripped and beaten with rods. After they had been severely flogged, they were thrown into prison ...
Acts 16:22-23

"Where, O death, is your victory? Where, O death, is your sting?"
1 Cor 15:55

I face death every day ...
1 Cor 15:31

...in great endurance; in troubles, hardships and distresses; in beatings, imprisonments and riots; in hard work, sleepless nights and hunger; in purity, understanding, patience and kindness; in the Holy Spirit and in sincere love; in truthful speech and in the power of God; with weapons of righteousness in the right hand and in the left; through glory and dishonor, bad report and good report; genuine, yet regarded as impostors; known, yet regarded as unknown; dying, and yet we live on; beaten, and yet not killed; sorrowful, yet always rejoicing; poor, yet making many rich; having nothing, and yet possessing everything.
2 Cor 6:4-10

...I have worked much harder, been in prison more frequently, been flogged more severely, and been exposed to death again and again. Five times I received from the Jews the forty lashes minus one. Three times I was beaten with rods, once I was pelted with stones, three times I was shipwrecked, I spent a night and a day in the open sea, I have been constantly on the move. I have been in danger from rivers, in danger from bandits, in danger from my fellow Jews, in danger from Gentiles; in danger in the city, in danger in the country, in danger at sea; and in danger from false believers. I have labored and toiled and have often gone without sleep; I have known hunger and thirst and have often gone without food; I have been cold and naked. Besides everything else, I face daily the pressure of my concern for all the churches.
2 Cor 11:23-28

If we live, we live for the Lord; and if we die, we die for the Lord... Romans 14:8

Join with me in suffering, like a good soldier of Christ Jesus.
2 Tim 2:3

...I was given a thorn in my flesh, a messenger of Satan, to torment me.
2 Cor 12:7

...Satan blocked our way.
1 Thess 2:18

Alexander the metalworker did me a great deal of harm ...
2 Tim 4:14

...I have finished the race, I have kept the faith.
2 Tim 4:7

Amazingly, Paul referred to his troubles as light and momentary![40]

Starting at entry level, sacrifice can be reflected in our worship—the fruit of our lips—because true worship means saying to God, or singing to God, what we truly mean, or *truly want* to truly mean!

> *Through Jesus, therefore, let us continually offer to God a sacrifice of praise—the fruit of lips that openly profess His name.* Hebrews 13:15

Singing a praise or worship song has no sacrificial value in itself unless it reflects a surrendered and thankful heart. Singing, *'I Surrender All'* without the slightest intention of truly wanting to surrender all would not be a precious sacrifice of praise, but merely a song. How often do I see God's people stare at the words in a book or on a screen and self–consciously mumble something to the music? How often have I seen men stand, clearly inwardly uncomfortable, with hands in pockets as they sing? Thanksgiving, which is the act of simply but sincerely saying 'Thank You' to God, is often the pathway that leads on to true praise and then to worship.[41] (I heard a man once say, 'Praise dances but worship kneels.')

Many things—especially the current events in our lives that seem to demand our attention — have the potential to rob of us of a thankful and worshipful heart. So, determine to ignore these events for a while. They will probably be waiting for you when you go back to them!

Lay your self–conscious self–image down. It's getting in the way! Set your culture aside. It's interfering! And just bring your thanksgiving to the Lord.

If that proves to be difficult, try this. Start to quietly give Him thanks for the things you probably take for granted. As you are reading these words, it is obvious you are blessed with sight. Close your eyes for a moment and imagine what it would be like to be blind. Then open your

Give thanks even in adverse circumstances and you will find yourself wonderfully enmeshed in God's will.

> When we bring the sacrifice of our time it should be the best of our free time, not the leftovers.

eyes and thank Him for the miracle that is your sight!

Imagine deafness for a moment. Then suddenly you hear birdsong, people's laughter and conversation. Give thanks. Imagine being unable to speak. But suddenly you can talk, and laugh, and sing. Give thanks. Can you walk? Give thanks. Can you taste food with your thousands of taste buds? Give thanks. Have you family and friends? Give thanks. You get the idea. Thanksgiving will arise deep within you, praise will follow and worship in spirit and truth will start to bubble forth.[42] Give thanks even in adverse circumstances and you will find yourself wonderfully enmeshed in God's will.

> *Give thanks in **all** circumstances; for this is God's will for you in Christ Jesus.* 1 Thessalonians 5:18 [emphasis mine]

However, worship in its fullness is more than the fruit of our lips. It outworks into action.[43] A fulfilled Christian life entails sacrificial service for Jesus at some level, and this involves a sacrifice of time. Worship and serving God are closely connected as different translations of this one verse illustrate.

> *Then the Lord said to Moses, "Get up early in the morning, confront Pharaoh and say to him, 'This is what the Lord, the God of the Hebrews, says: "Let My people go, so that they may **worship Me**."* Exodus 9:13 [emphasis mine]

> *Then the Lord said to Moses, "Rise early in the morning and stand before Pharaoh, and say to him, 'Thus says the Lord God of the Hebrews: "Let My people go, that they may **serve Me**."* Exodus 9:13 NKJV bv [emphasis mine]

Throughout Scripture a sacrifice had to be without blemish.[44] The best of the flock. No broken or damaged animals. (Hence the Lamb of God without blemish.[45]) When we bring the sacrifice of our time it should be the best of our free time, not the leftovers. In our available free time we follow our heart,[46] and giving Jesus the seconds or thirds does not constitute sacrifice. When you know you are truly, totally and deeply God's beloved son or daughter, then all sacrificial service is a delight. A privilege. An honor. A response compelled by love.[47] Otherwise it is just cold duty. If the latter is you please read my first book.[48]

Then there is our money. Our hard-earned money. So many Christians struggle to truly sacrifice here. Often we just give God our spare change. However sacrifice, by its very nature, hurts and involves a cost to ourselves. King David described the principle:

> But the king replied to Araunah, "No, I insist on paying you for it. I will not sacrifice to the Lord my God burnt offerings **that cost me nothing**." So David bought the threshing floor and the oxen and paid fifty shekels of silver for them. 2 Samuel 24:24 [emphasis mine]

Some Christians tithe. Many choose not to, or do not believe that in the New Covenant it even needs to be considered. I personally think Jesus affirmed it when He rebuked the religious Pharisees for tithing but ignoring concern for people.

> "Woe to you, teachers of the law and Pharisees, you hypocrites! *You give a tenth* of your spices – mint, dill and cumin. But you have neglected the more important matters of the law – justice, mercy and faithfulness. You should have practiced the latter, *without neglecting the former.* Matthew 23:23 [emphasis mine]

If a tenth was the Old Covenant rule of thumb then I would not want to give Jesus less. That money goes to support Kingdom work.[49] Alms to the poor and needy is additional.[50] And God honoring. Moving on with God is the opposite to being stationary. Adventure involves challenge and challenge involves a measure of fear. No change means that nothing changes. God has plans for us all. For some it will mean serving Him in what might seem small and unseen ways. Unseen by men perhaps, but not unseen. The ornate pillars at the front of Solomon's temple had ornamental pomegranates in bowls set on the very top where no man could see them.[51] *But God could see them.* Some sacrificial service beautifully garnishes the pillars and is visible to all and appreciated by many. But some sacrificial service garnishes the very top of the pillars where only He sees. And that's enough. We are God's co–workers, and He is no man's debtor.[52]

Some probing questions.

- Is this the first time you have heard about the sacrificial lifestyle?

- Do you see the beauty of the sacrificial lifestyle?

- Can you think of any personal sacrifice in your current Christian walk?

- Who has influenced you through their sacrificial lifestyle?

THREE
How to Boil a Frog?

A strange title for a chapter, but it will soon make sense!

When I was a little boy I spent all school holidays at my grandmother's home near the seaside.

It was a simple home—like many of its day. No inside toilet. No electricity. Gas mantles and candles provided light when evening came. Rooms were tiny and stairs were steep. The kitchen was very humble. A white stone sink with one tap for cold water. A curtain round the base of the sink provided a storage place where pots and pans were kept out of sight. There was a crude worktop with stick–on washproof covering and above the worktop two wooden shelves for plates and cups. A gas cooker completed the setup.

On the top shelf there was one item that was only for show. A jug with handles on either side. It had a simple little flower painted on the front but inside it held a secret. At the bottom of the jug, as if hiding away, was a lifelike porcelain frog. Many times I asked my father if I could look inside the jug to see if the frog was still there and then asking him if the frog could get out. It was during one of these times he explained to me that, if you put a frog in a pot of cold water and very gently heated it, the frog would never jump out. Eventually the hot water would kill it. *Frogs are stupid*, I thought.

> Despite the awful effects of the fall there is still a stamp of righteousness permanently within man.

As I got older I lost interest in the porcelain frog. My maturing imagination refused to let me believe it was real. But I never forgot the story my father told me about a frog in a pot.

Recently I decided to see if the story was real. I watched a video of a man testing the theory and it is true.[53] As the water heats up gradually the frog adjusts to the slightly warmer temperature and remains comfortable. If the water heats up too quickly the frog recognizes the impending danger and leaps out to safety.

I'm sure you can already see where this is going.

Three times Jesus referred to the devil as the 'prince of this world'.[54]

The apostle Paul referred to him as 'the ruler of the kingdom of the air'[55] and the 'god of this world'.[56] He called his dominion 'the dominion of darkness'.[57] The apostle John declared that the whole world lies under his evil sway.[58]

And indeed it does. His fingerprints are everywhere, but—because we are all made in God's image[59]—despite the awful effects of the fall there is still a stamp of righteousness permanently within man.[60] Even when a sin–hardened man is subjected to a lie detector test, it can usually register a reaction when he tells a lie.

God says, "This is the way, walk in it."[61] God says, "I set before you blessing and curse, life and death, chose life!"[62] "Life in abundance."[63] "Freedom!"[64]

The devil says God's way is bondage and that self–rule is the real way to freedom.[65] Always hiding the fact that self–rule is his rule.[66]

To lead mankind deeper into his dominion of darkness, the devil needs to convince us there is no danger in the direction we are heading. Sadly many people need little convincing, but others, sensing something of that stamp of righteousness within themselves are harder to lead in that direction.

One of the devil's descriptions is 'deceiver'[67] and he is good at it.

He knows how to boil a frog.

If society rejects certain behavior it locks the moral temperature at that point so he needs to influence their thinking slowly, gradually, step by step. In 1931 the British Broadcasting Corporation (BBC) unveiled a plaque in the entrance hall of their headquarters at BBC Broadcasting House, Portland Place, London, declaring aims very much in tune with mainstream society at that time:

> "To Almighty God, this shrine of the arts, music and literature is dedicated by the first Governors in the year of our Lord 1931, John Reith being Director General. It is their prayer that good seed sown will produce a good harvest, that everything offensive to decency and hostile to peace will be expelled, and that the nation will incline its ear to those things which are lovely, pure and of good report and thus pursue that path of wisdom and virtue."

Seventy–five years later that God–honoring vision had changed out of all recognition. In 2004 they aired the grossly blasphemous and foul–mouthed *Jerry Springer—the opera*. It was so offensive that, for the first time in years, the public—and especially Christians—were roused to publicly protest in substantial numbers.[68] A record number of nearly 63,000 people complained, but the BBC chose to ignore such a protest,[69] and Ofcom—the government communications regulator also rejected the complaints. The temperature of society's moral water had dramatically changed. But not quickly. Gradually.

The 'god of this world' has brought society to a place where it is reveling in, and even celebrating, its fallen state.

The 'god of this world' has brought society to a place where it is reveling in, and even celebrating, its fallen state. Calling it freedom rather than desperately seeking God's face for freedom from it!

When I was a young man, swearing in public would have been unthinkable and unacceptable. Then in 1965 Kenneth Tynan used the infamous 'f' word on the BBC and there was an outcry.[70] Today television, cinema and public life is awash with swearing. The moral temperature has changed. Gradually.

When I was a young man the idea of sexual promiscuity being mentioned in public was so unthinkable that, in 1967, most radio stations banned the *Rolling Stones* song *Let's spend the night together* and played the B–side *Ruby Tuesday* instead. In the USA, Ed Sullivan would not permit the *Stones* to sing that line on his show, saying, "Either the song goes or you go." As a compromise, the words were changed to "Let's spend some time together." However as Mick Jagger sang that line he rolled his eyes, causing Ed Sullivan to say they would never again appear on his show.[71]

Now most films, much TV content and many songs glorify blatant sexual promiscuity. The moral temperature has changed. Gradually.

When I was a young man, pornography was regarded as gross immorality. Now pornography is so deeply embedded into society it has larger revenues than Microsoft, Google, Amazon, eBay, Yahoo, Apple and Netflix combined.[72] A UK survey showed that four out of five sixteen–year olds regularly view pornography online, while one in every three ten–year olds have viewed similar images.[73] The moral temperature has changed. Gradually.

When I was a young man, society regarded witchcraft as a bad thing. Occult activities in all forms were to be avoided. Witches and their supernatural spells were always portrayed as bad in everything from *Macbeth* to *The Chronicles of Narnia*. In recent decades, television's portrayal of witches has changed that. In 1964, in *Bewitched*, good witch Samantha could twitch her nose and the supernatural would bring events into line with her will. Then in the late 90s there was *Charmed* where three sisters used their witchcraft against the evil forces, and *Sabrina the Teenage Witch* who, while learning her craft, often saw her spells go wrong. Thus society was ready for the *Harry Potter* 'good witchcraft versus bad witchcraft' phenomenon. While on holiday in Scotland some years ago, and visiting one of their many great castles, I was shocked to see booklets on spells and voodoo kits for sale in the tearoom alongside traditional Scottish tourist offerings. The moral temperature has changed. Gradually.

When I was a young man, society could never have been envisioned marriage as being anything other than a man and woman, but today men are getting married to men and women to women.[74] The moral temperature has changed. Gradually.

Abortion, which was legalized for medical reasons, gradually degenerated into abortion on demand.[75] The womb was always meant to be a safe place, but now, as Arthur Francis Green said in his book, *When Fables Fall*, *"It works out that, statistically, one of the most dangerous places to be in the UK is in the womb."* In the first ten years of this new century the average abortion rate has reached nearly twenty–three percent, or put this way, every fifth pregnancy is aborted.[76] To put real numbers to this slaughter of the innocents, between 1968 and 2010 the number of *legal* abortions in England and Wales alone was 7,003,416.[77] The changes just keep coming. Gradually.

Euthanasia and assisted suicide—already legal in some countries—is under pressure to be made legal in the UK and elsewhere. Its introduction is being argued for on behalf of those are suffering greatly and whose quality of life is virtually non–existent. However, past experience shows that, like abortion, once it is legalized for genuine acts of human mercy, it will gradually degenerate into abuse. In the UK the 'Liverpool Care Pathway' had to be abolished in 2013[78] because it had degenerated into an '*assisted death pathway rather than a care pathway.*' A leading NHS Professor said, *"If we accept the Liverpool Care Pathway we accept that euthanasia is part of the standard way of dying as it is now associated with 29 per cent of NHS deaths."*[79] The changes will keep coming. Gradually.

> Many Christians have been unaware 'the god of this world' is slowly boiling them.

The last moral barrier, pedophilia, is under pressure to move boundary lines. Traditionally a pedophile was a person who had sexual contact with a minor—a person under the legal age of consent. The age of consent varies from country to country and in the UK and the USA it is set at the age of sixteen. However, with the sexualisation of young children through constant exposure to sexual images and lyrics,[80] coupled with a reported lowering age for the onset of puberty,[81] the sexual behavior of young people has undergone a dramatic change. A 1994 survey in the USA revealed that twenty–three percent of all 14–year–olds and 30 percent of all 15–year–olds have had sexual intercourse.[82] Two decades later one can only imagine what today's figures might be. In England's Southampton, nine schools have offered contraceptive implants to young girls through their sexual health clinics. In 2012 NHS figures showed that one thousand seven hundred girls aged thirteen and fourteen had the implants fitted.[83] With such changes taking place and on a rising scale, it is no surprise that pressure is increasing to lower the age of consent to the age of 13[84] or 14.[85] In certain circles pedophilia is now being described as 'minor-attracted people' [86] or 'intergenerational relationships' with claims it is misunderstood.[87] Using the same tactics as gay rights activists, pedophiles have begun to seek similar status arguing that their desire for children is a sexual orientation no different from hetrosexual or homosexuals.[88] In 2006, a Dutch court refused to ban a new political party with a pedophile agenda. The judge said the *Brotherly Love, Freedom and Diversity Party* (PNVD) had the same right to exist as any other political party. The declared aim of this new party is to break the 'negative' stigma surrounding pedophilia by getting into parliament.[89] Today, its offensive agenda will have little success, but, as with the other issues mentioned, it puts the subject and alternative views on the table. In the coming years I have little doubt the moral temperature on this issue will change.[90] Gradually.

The devil knows how to boil a frog. Many Christians have been unaware 'the god of this world' is slowly boiling them. That's why friendship with the world is enmity with God.[91] Too often we are lulled into thinking that, as long as we stay a few steps behind the moral movement, we are not affected.

But moving we are. The level of sin in the church at present is shocking. Especially in the area of sexual immorality.[92] But few are shocked. The media has soaked us all in sinful behavior and we now see much of it as normal behavior. We have quietly adjusted to the new temperature. We have changed. Gradually.

It's as though the walls of Jerusalem are broken, the gates are burnt,[93] and the people within the walls go walkabout outside while the people outside come walkabout inside. There is little difference in worldview and behavior between saved and unsaved. Today, like the unredeemed, we let ourselves be entertained by the things that sent Jesus to the cross.[94]

If a Christian arose from a fifty–year coma he would be shocked and distressed by the dramatic changes in society's morality, because unlike us, he would not have been able to adjust to the changes gradually.

As Christians we are called to be salt and light in an ever–darkening world.[95]

If we have lost our saltiness, what use are we to Christ as witnesses, as living letters and as ambassadors for His Kingdom?[96]

We are called to be light, to reflect The Light, and to shine brightly in the gathering spiritual and moral darkness.[97] We were chosen in Christ before the creation of the world to be holy and blameless in His sight.[98]

Our righteousness comes from being clothed with the Righteousness of Christ. However our part is to actively cooperate with the Holy Spirit within us in order to work out, or out–work, that Kingdom culture in our day–to–day living.[99] The apostle Paul described Kingdom culture this way:

> *Finally, brothers and sisters, whatever is true, whatever is noble, whatever is right, whatever is pure, whatever is lovely, whatever is*

> When we gradually conform to the ever–changing pattern of this world we lose spiritual discernment.

admirable—if anything is excellent or praiseworthy—think about such things. Philippians 4:8

Why would we give God less than our best? Oswald Chambers put it well with the title of his famous devotional book, *My Utmost for His Highest.* We are a chosen people, a royal priesthood, a holy nation, and God's special possession.[100] Listen to heaven's call.

"'Come out from them and be separate,' says the Lord. 'Touch no unclean thing, and I will receive you. And, I will be a Father to you, and you will be my sons and daughters,' says the Lord Almighty." 2 Corinthians 6:17–18

We belong to and represent a different Kingdom. Christ's Kingdom. A Kingdom that is not an alternative culture, but a contra–culture. We must choose.

Do not love the world or the things in the world. If anyone loves the world, the love of the Father is not in him. For all that is in the world, the lust of the flesh, the lust of the eyes, and the pride of life, is not of the Father, but is of the world. 1 John 2:15–16

God does not do mixtures.[101] Scripture rightly asks, *"How can two walk together unless they agree?"* [102] We can have the mind of Christ or the mind of secular society. When we gradually conform to the ever–changing pattern of this world we lose spiritual discernment. And it is harder, perhaps impossible, to know God's perfect will for our lives. He loves us passionately, but He will not bless what He cannot bless.

Do not conform any longer to the pattern of this world, but be transformed by the renewing of your mind. Then you will be able to test and approve what God's will is—His good, pleasing and perfect will. Romans 12:2

The good news is that the Father—who loves us so much that He sent His only–begotten Son to die for us—has given us His written promise that, if we submit to Him and acknowledge Him in all our ways, He will direct our paths.[103]

Don't be a frog. *Be a disciple.*

Some probing questions:

- What do you choose to watch that Jesus would not watch with you?

- Which ways do you realize that you been slowly boiled over the years?

- What changes do you see happening in society today?

- How will you react to this chapter?

FOUR
The Value of a Soul

This is a short chapter—less than 1000 words—but an important chapter to follow on from the previous one.

People's minds, the apostle Paul said, are blinded and influenced by 'the god of this age'.[104] Thus, as described in the last chapter, some of their behavior reflects this. But listen. Before we were saved, so did ours. Once we did this and that and 'the other thing'. Listen to the apostle Paul again as he confirms this:

> *Or do you not know that wrongdoers will not inherit the kingdom of God? Do not be deceived: Neither the sexually immoral nor idolaters nor adulterers nor men who have sex with men, nor thieves nor the greedy nor drunkards nor slanderers nor swindlers will inherit the kingdom of God.* ***And that is what some of you were.*** *But you were washed, you were sanctified, you were justified in the name of the Lord Jesus Christ and by the Spirit of our God.* 1 Corinthians 6:9–11 [emphasis mine]

When we were doing this and that and the other thing, God placed great value on our soul. Great value.

So much value in fact that while we were sinners He sent His Son to die for us so that a way could be made for us to come home to Him.[105] To be His children, His sons and His daughters.[106]

Only when the blindfold is removed from our minds and our spirit fused with God's Spirit can we begin to understand the great value God places on us as individuals.[107]

Here's the lesson in moving on with God.

We are to see the great value in everyone else's soul. Despite fallen language and fallen behavior and anti–Christian sentiments, we are to see the great value God has placed on their souls.

We are all made in God's image. We are all individuals. We all have worth.

I have had the immeasurable privilege of ministering in word and prayer to men who were drug addicts, drug dealers, violent men, gang members. And I have seen Jesus transform some of these men into passionate disciples and close friends. The veil was taken away. They came alive in Him.

Jesus calls us out of the world and its ways, then sends us into all the world to be His witness. To show what life lived under His Lordship is like. To show what it is like to be loved to the core of our being by His Father, and now *our* Father.

Don't be like the religious Pharisees who dragged the woman caught in adultery before Jesus, certain He had to condemn her. He could have—because what she did was sinful. But He didn't. He stooped down and wrote in the sand with his finger. Scripture doesn't say what He wrote but I think it is obvious He began writing the 'secret sins' of those Pharisees because, convicted by their conscience, one by one they turned and silently left the scene. Jesus did not come to condemn, He came to save. However as the grateful woman left that dreadful scene Jesus said to her: *"Go now and leave your life of sin."* [108]

That adulterous woman could be anyone with any particular sin you can think of. Our call is to love the sinner, but not the sin.

Condemning might work sometimes, but Scripture tells us: *'Love never fails.'*[109]

Jesus' sacrificial death is not sufficient for just some of us. It has been made available for the entire world.

> *He is the atoning sacrifice for our sins, and not only for ours but also for the sins of **the whole world**.* 1 John 2:2 [emphasis mine]

It is no accident that this is the world's best–known Scripture:

> *For God so **loved the world** that he gave his one and only Son, that whoever believes in Him shall not perish but have eternal life.* John 3:16 [emphasis mine]

That's why we are called to go into the entire world with the good news.[110] To be His witnesses. Only when we see the value of each soul can we truly represent God's heart.

I know from Scripture that it is God's heart that none should perish.[111] We are called to love the unlovable, because He once loved unlovable us. We are called to love the least of them.[112] Jesus modeled it for us. He loved the unclean leper, the crooked tax collectors, the rough and ready fishermen, the poor, the lame, the blind, the demonized, you, and me.

> Only when we see the value of each soul can we truly represent God's heart.

We are called to love our neighbor.[113] "Ah!" you say, "that's easy, I have lovely neighbors." Me too. But that next–door neighbor was not what Jesus was talking about as He made very clear in His parable of the Good Samaritan.[114] The Jews and the Samaritans hated each other; wanted nothing to do with each other.[115] They didn't even want to walk through each other's territory, but the Good Samaritan was the one who helped his Jewish 'neighbor'.

Put on God glasses and look around. The fields are white unto harvest![116]

Some probing questions:

- Who is the first unlovable person that comes to mind?

- Have you, or will you make a start by praying for them?

- Was there a time when you were unlovable?

FIVE
Electrifying Faith!

Pause for a moment and look at an electric light bulb in your room. (I'll wait while you look!) You don't need to be an electrician to know it usually has two thin wires that feed power into it. Those wires can be traced along a national grid all the way back to a mighty power station, probably many, many miles away. Power flows day and night from that power station through the wires and, at the flick of a switch the light bulb lights up. Wow—where there was darkness, now there is light!

If you were a terrorist (please don't be!) and you wanted to put out this light in your room, you could do one of two things. You could try and destroy the mighty power station many, many miles away, or, you could just snip one of the thin wires attached to the bulb's light fitting. Either way the light goes out. The terrorist's choice would be obvious. Cut the thin wire that feeds the power directly into the light bulb. Easy! Job done. Move on.

Now imagine for a moment you are the light bulb, designed to shine brightly in the darkness of this world,[117] and that God Almighty—Father Son and Holy Spirit[118]—is that great power station.[119] Your faith is the invisible wiring that links the two. When *by faith* you were born again,[120] the light switch was flicked on as your spirit suddenly came alive to God. Through this link of faith, God's Mighty Power–through the Person of the

Holy Spirit[121]– flowed into your spirit, enabling you to begin your new life as a child of God.

> *But as many as received Him, to them He gave the right to become children of God, to those who believe on His name.* John 1:12 NKJV

Type the words 'by faith' into your computer's Bible program or an online Bible search website and you will see nearly fifty verses for the New International Version. Here's a sample [with the emphasis mine]…

> … *"The righteous will live **by faith**."* Romans 1:17

> …*therefore, the promise comes **by faith**…* Romans 4:16

> …*through whom we have gained access **by faith** into this grace…* Romans 5:2

> …*they were broken off because of unbelief, and you stand **by faith**…* Romans 11:20

> …*because it is **by faith** you stand firm.* 2 Corinthians 1:24

> *For we live **by faith**, not by sight.* 2 Corinthians 5:7

> ***By faith** we understand that the universe was formed at God's command…* Hebrews 11:3

Jesus often pointed out to a person that their faith had played an important part in their healing. Here's a sample [with the emphasis mine]…

> *"Take heart, daughter,"* he said, *"**your faith** has healed you."* Matthew 9:22

> *"According to **your faith** let it be done to you."* Matthew 9:29

> *"**Your faith** has saved you; go in peace."* Luke 7:50

> *"Rise and go; **your faith** has made you well."* Luke 17:19

The apostle Paul wrote that faith comes by hearing the word of God.[122] Now understand that Satan is the spiritual terrorist who hates God and hates everyone and everything that God loves. This fallen one, once called Lucifer[123] but now called the devil,[124] desperately—but cunningly and patiently—wants to extinguish or diminish your God–given light. He has two options. Try and destroy God Almighty[125] in the highest heaven,[126] or, simply cut your faith. His choice is obvious. Cut your faith, or gradually thin it down to 'little faith'.[127] Does that make sense?

Where the physical terrorist would use wire cutters the spiritual terrorist uses doubt.

Remember his recorded tactics way back in the first pages of Genesis. *"Did God really say…?"* [128] Remember his tactics with Jesus, the Last Adam? *"If you are the Son of God…"* [129]

The battle is real. Many realize they have lost their first love.[130] Lost that spark, that electrifying faith that was there when they first believed.

Many realize that where they were once hot they are now lukewarm.[131]

They know they are saved and their names safely written in the Lamb's book of Life,[132] yet with no electrifying faith to empower them. To let them shine.[133] To discover their calling and their destiny on earth.[134]

If that describes you, then check what the serpent has done to the wiring of your faith. Don't be offended when I suggest this. Put your Bible on the floor and stand on it.

Now say, *"Lord, I am standing on your Word, and I will not be moved off it.*[135] *There is much I do not yet understand, but I do know that your Word is truth. That your Word is a lamp unto my feet and a light unto my path"* [136]

Now try this. Hold the Bible immediately over your head and say, *"Lord I choose to shelter under your Word. To live under the authority of your Word. To let your Word rule and judge my life for your glory."*

Now this. Hold the Bible next to your heart. "Lord, I choose to hide your Word in my heart so that it may be the directing power in my life."[137]

"Lord, I present my life to you. I lay it on the altar as a living sacrifice to you alone. I ask you to help me not to conform to the pressures of this world, but to be transformed by the renewing of my mind." [138]

Every morning make sure your heart is an open channel to God. Check for any seeds of unbelief. And every evening do business with God to ensure there is no undealt–with sin that has clouded your heart,[139] the receiver of His power.

Be filled with His Spirit, and stay filled with His Spirit!

Some probing questions:

- Can you remember how you felt when you first came alive on to God?

- If ten is 'radically on fire for Jesus' and one is 'stone cold', where would you grade yourself today?

- Has anything, or anybody, undermined your faith?

SIX
Would You Believe It?

'that we should no longer be children, tossed to and fro and carried about with every wind of doctrine...' Ephesians 4:14

For some, this may be the most challenging chapter of all! It's about putting down roots—strong doctrinal roots—into the Word of God, because sadly, there is a rapidly developing slide towards apostasy within the Body of Christ. Like a great whale being savaged by hundreds of hungry sharks, each taking just one bite, the integrity and thus *the authority* of Scripture is being relentlessly attacked by atheists and liberal theologians alike. Yes, we keep talking about Jesus and the cross and our forgiveness and so on—the crux of the faith—but the *vital foundational doctrines* that God underpins the gospel with have almost gone.

The result is that Christians have been greatly fragmented in their beliefs, and rendered powerless in confidence and authority. Some are dangerously on the edge of the faith. Some have, I suspect, left the faith but still talk as though they have not.

I pray that this chapter will provide you with a strong Scriptural plumbline. It is the one I live by.

The word 'doctrine' is mentioned more than thirty times in the New Testament (New King James Version), so its importance cannot be overstated. Based on the traditional premise that Scripture is truth, there are many issues of interpretation over which we can, and do, 'legally' argue and debate[140] (hence the different denominations). However clear main-frame Biblical doctrine is not something we can choose to ignore, add to, take away from or twist out of shape. We have two choices set before us. We can accept it or reject it.

Paul wrote to the church at Corinth:

> *Examine yourselves to see whether you are in the faith; test yourselves. Do you not realize that Christ Jesus is in you—unless, of course, you fail the test?* 2 Corinthians 13:5

That is a serious challenge. How would we test ourselves to see if we are still in the faith? The obvious answer is that our faith's integrity is based on the Person of Jesus Christ. God incarnate. *If we, the Body of Christ here on earth, do not believe what Jesus believes, then there is a problem.*

Just speaking about, or singing to, or praying to someone whom you refer to as Jesus does not mean that you are interacting with Immanuel— *'God with us'* [141]—as revealed in scripture.

For instance, the 'Jesus' that Jehovah's Witnesses speak of is Michael the Archangel, whom they say God adopted as His son at the river Jordan. The Mormon's 'Jesus' is a son born out of a physical sexual relationship between God the Father—who is a resurrected man with a physical body, who has a Father God above him—and Mary, with no involvement of the Holy Spirit. The Muslim 'Jesus' was born to Mary as the result of virginal conception and was given power by God to perform miracles to aid him in his ministry, but the Muslim 'Jesus' is not God incarnate, nor the Son of God, but

> We are called to believe what Jesus believes, but so often we are strongly influenced by the current wisdom of the world.

a mortal man, a Muslim prophet, a messenger of Allah, and a precursor to the prophet Mohammed. Then there is the Hindu 'Jesus', the Buddhist 'Jesus', the Bahá'i 'Jesus', the Rastafarian 'Jesus', the Unitarian 'Jesus', the Christadelphian 'Jesus', the Christian Science 'Jesus', the Unification ('Moonies') 'Jesus', the New Age 'Jesus' and the Esoteric 'Jesus'.

You get the idea.

How do we know for certain that none of these are the real Jesus? We apply the plumbline of Scripture. The Jesus we worship, the Jesus we follow MUST BE Jesus the Messiah as revealed in Scripture. He is the Word become flesh.[142] All Christians must surely say *amen* to that.

So—if Jesus believed something that later proved to be untrue then He could not be 'The Truth'.[143] He could not be God.[144] He could not be The Messiah. He could not be The Lord of Lords. All Christians must surely say *amen* to that. We are called to believe what Jesus believes,[145] but so often we are strongly influenced by the *current* wisdom of the world.[146] The result is that we can gradually compromise our beliefs and subtly shape 'our Jesus' into a person who believes what *we now choose to believe*. Therefore we can end up worshipping ourselves when we worship a 'Jesus' made in our own image, since 'our Jesus' is at peace with *our* beliefs, rather than we with His. I hope that makes sense!

A very large number of people who claim to follow Jesus, including many leaders, believe that creation events as recorded in the opening chapters of Genesis are poetic, figurative or symbolic. They see the record of Scripture as not necessarily historical or, if historical, then with extra–biblical add–ons inserted between Genesis 1:1 and 1:2. Thus a growing a–la–carte menu of Genesis theologies is now available to Christians, such as day–age,[147] gap,[148] soft gap,[149] framework hypothesis,[150] theistic evolution,[151] revelatory day[152] and progressive creation.[153] Some of these theologies introduce us to ideas such as a soulless pre–Adamic race,[154] 'Lucifer's flood' and a previous creation ruined and then re–created,[155] with death and disease in operation before the fall of man.[156]

There are, almost certainly, poetic, figurative and symbolic aspects to the opening chapters of Genesis (e.g. the tree of the knowledge of good and evil[157]) but we must not be too hasty in rejecting the historical aspect. Scripture is wonderfully knit together, so we must be careful to ensure we stay within safe doctrinal boundaries of Biblical creation, otherwise, *as will be seen*, by knocking down one little 'domino' at the beginning, we start a mighty chain reaction throughout Scripture.

For instance, a very large number of people who claim to follow Jesus, including many leaders, have decided there never was a historical Adam and Eve. However—by quoting from Genesis 1:27 and then in His next sentence quoting Genesis 2:24 verbatim—Jesus confirmed (albeit indirectly) they were indeed *a very real couple* who were created at the beginning of creation.[158] No less than five of the New Testament books also refer to Adam, or to Adam and Eve, as real historical people.[159]

Dr. Albert Mohler, president of one of the world's largest seminaries, *The Southern Baptist Theological Seminary*, writes, "The denial of a historical Adam and Eve as the first parents of all humanity and the solitary first human pair severs the link between Adam and Christ which is so crucial to the Gospel."[160]

Sadly, atheists understand the argument surrounding the literal reality of Adam and Eve better than many Christians.

Atheist Frank Zindler said,

> "Now that we know that Adam and Eve never were real people the central myth of Christianity is destroyed. If there never was an Adam and Eve there never was an original sin. If there never was an original sin there is no need of salvation. If there is no need of salvation there is no need of a saviour. And I submit that puts Jesus, historical or otherwise, into the ranks of the unemployed. I think that evolution is absolutely the death knell of Christianity."[161]

Atheist Richard Bozarth said,

"...evolution destroys utterly and finally the very reason Jesus' earthly life was supposedly made necessary. Destroy Adam and Eve and the original sin, and in the rubble you will find the sorry remains of the Son of God. If Jesus was not the redeemer who died for our sins, and this is what evolution means, then Christianity is nothing."[162]

I deal with evolution in some detail in my first book.[163] If you believe that evolution is a fact, rather than a working hypothesis, I would earnestly advise spending quality time on the thousands of articles now available on the many excellent creation websites[164] or reading some of the superb books which respond scientifically.[165]

The New Testament has more than 100 quotations or direct references to the first eleven chapters of Genesis[166] and all the major foundational Christian doctrines are rooted in the early chapters of Genesis. So when you declare those chapters to be steeped in unreality, you abandon the foundations of essential Biblical doctrine. The dominoes begin to topple, each one knocking down another in the chain.

For instance, why did Jesus have to die on the cross? Because of Adam's sin.

> *For as in Adam all die, so in Christ all will be made alive.* 1 Corinthians 15:22

Christian foundational doctrine is that sin entered through one man— Adam—and was dealt with by God through the grace of one man, Jesus.

> *For if the many died by the trespass of the one man, how much more did God's grace and the gift that came by the grace of the one man, Jesus Christ, overflow to the many!* Romans 5:15

Thus if you deny the reality of the first Adam, you can longer claim the 'Jesus' you worship and follow is the Last Adam. Scripture will simply not permit them be separated.

> *So it is written: "The first man Adam became a living being," the last Adam, a life-giving spirit.* 1 Corinthians 15:45

A 'Jesus' divorced from any links to the first Adam is not the Jesus revealed in Scripture or the Jesus *that Paul preached*. Thus the Spirit of God is not the spirit behind such a doctrine.

> *For if someone comes to you and preaches a Jesus other than the Jesus we preached, or if you receive a different spirit from the Spirit you received, or a different gospel from the one you accepted, you put up with it easily enough.* 2 Corinthians 11:4

A very large number of people who claim to follow Jesus, including many leaders, have decided to believe God did not flood the whole earth covering 'all the high mountains under the entire heavens' as described in the Bible.[167] It is, they believe, myth, perhaps based on stories of a local flood.

Yet in Matthew 24:37–39, Jesus refers to Noah, the ark, and the great flood. Clearly He believed this event to be truth. And of course still does so today.[168]

A very large number of people who claim to follow Jesus, including many leaders, have decided to believe the Genesis 19 story of God destroying Sodom and Gomorrah was a myth. Yet in Luke 17:28–30, Jesus refers to the raining down of fire and brimstone that wrought destruction on Sodom and Gomorrah. Clearly He believed this event to be truth. Peter, who spent three years in the close company of Jesus, confirmed both the flood and the destruction of Sodom and Gomorrah.[169]

A very large number of people who claim to follow Jesus, including many leaders, have decided that Jonah being swallowed by a large fish is mythical.

Yet in Matthew 12:40, Jesus not only refers to Jonah and the three days and three nights that he spent in the belly of the great fish, but uses it as a sign of His coming resurrection. Clearly He believed this event to be truth. And still does.

Moses is mentioned some 38 times in the gospels alone with Jesus referring to him 19 times. We read where Jesus spoke with Moses (and Elijah) face to face on the Mount of Transfiguration.

Even after His resurrection, on the road to Emmaus, Jesus expounded the Scriptures beginning with Moses. There is little doubt He would have begun by referring to what Moses wrote about Him in Genesis chapter three—the first, and arguably one of the most important of the Messianic prophecies, where God addressed the serpent (Satan[170]):

> *"And I will put enmity between you and the woman, and between your offspring and hers; He will crush your head, and you will strike His heel."* Genesis 3:15

So much of the Bible, and therefore its integrity, is linked to Moses and of course the Ten Commandments written by the very Finger of God Himself on Mount Sinai. Jesus—directly and indirectly—often quoted from the Ten Commandments.[171] Just as Moses and the Old Testament are inseparable, so Moses and the New Testament are equally inseparable. Jesus said,

> *"If you believed Moses, you would believe Me, for he wrote about Me..."* John 5:46

Every Christian should and would say *amen* to that. *Or would they?*

The fourth commandment, written by the Finger of God Himself, contains this sentence.

> For **in six days the Lord made the heavens and the earth, the sea, and all that is in them**, but he rested on the seventh day. Therefore the Lord blessed the Sabbath day and made it holy. Exodus 20:11 [emphasis mine]

For emphasis this declaration is repeated in Exodus chapter thirty–one.

> *The Israelites are to observe the Sabbath, celebrating it for the generations to come as a lasting covenant. It will be a sign between me and the Israelites forever,* **for in six days the Lord made the heavens and the earth**, *and on the seventh day he rested and was refreshed. When the Lord finished speaking to Moses on Mount Sinai, he gave him the two tablets of the covenant law, the tablets of stone*

> ***inscribed by the finger of God.*** Exodus 31:16–18 [emphasis mine]

There is simply no escaping the fact that—engraved in stone—God was clearly, *and very precisely*, speaking of days *as we understand them*, and not in some mystical, 'one day you will understand' sense. If you do not believe that 'in six days the Lord made the heavens and the earth, the sea, and all that is in them,' then you would have to believe that Moses merely recycled a Babylonian myth, or simply made it up, and chipped the words on to the tablets himself, and so was nothing better than an ungodly deceiver.

However God declared to Israel that, with Moses—and Moses alone—He spoke *face to face*. Moses did not get his written accounts from a dream or a vision or an impression. He got them, along with the Ten Commandments, from God. Face to face.

> *"Listen to my words: When there is a prophet among you, I, the Lord, reveal myself to them in visions, I speak to them in dreams. But this is not true of my servant Moses; he is faithful in all my house.* **With him I speak face to face, clearly and not in riddles**; *he sees the form of the Lord. Why then were you not afraid to speak against my servant Moses?"* Numbers 12: 6–8 [emphasis mine]

So if God spoke to Moses face to face on Mount Sinai and His own finger wrote on the tablets of stone, then to hold to a contrary view, is to presume God got it wrong!

If *your* God got it wrong, if *your* Moses got it wrong, then *your* Jesus got it wrong. So the one whom you profess to worship is not The One who is clearly revealed in Scripture. Can you see how knocking down one domino starts a chain reaction?

Jesus taught that the entire Old Testament is divinely inspired.

> *He said to them, "This is what I told you while I was still with you: Everything must be fulfilled that is written about Me in the Law of Moses, the Prophets and the Psalms." Then He opened their minds so they could understand the Scriptures.* Luke 24:44–45

To quote the ESV Bible commentary,

> When the Bible says that "He opened their minds to understand the scriptures", it cannot mean just a few scattered predictions about the Messiah. It means the Old Testament as a whole, encompassing all three of the major divisions of the Old Testament that the Jews traditionally recognized. "The Law of Moses" includes Genesis to Deuteronomy. "The Prophets" include both the 'former prophets' (the historical books Joshua, Judges, 1–2 Samuel, and 1–2 Kings) and 'the latter prophets' (Isaiah, Jeremiah, Ezekiel, and the 12 minor prophets, Hosea – Malachi) 'The Psalms' is representative of the third groupings by the Jews called the 'Writings' (The book of Daniel was placed in this group)

Despite this clear teaching from Jesus, a very large number of people including many leaders have decided that the Old Testament in particular is awash with error.

Some Bibles put the spoken words of Jesus in red, visually locking His words into the gospels and the Book of Revelation alone. However John the beloved, the apostle closest to Jesus, declared under the inspiration of the Holy Spirit that Jesus is "The Word become flesh".[172] When John spoke that truth, the existing Word at that time was the Old Testament.

Indeed Jesus quoted from Genesis, Exodus, Leviticus, Deuteronomy, Psalms, Proverbs, Isaiah, Jeremiah, Ezekiel, Daniel, Hosea, Amos, Jonah, Micah and Malachi.

He referred to the Old Testament as "the scriptures", "the word of God" and "the wisdom of God".

Not one word of the New Testament gospels or epistles had yet been written when Jesus said that the Scriptures—thus referring to the Old Testament books—testified of Himself.

You study the Scriptures diligently because you think that in them you have eternal life. These are the very Scriptures that testify about Me.
John 5:39

Again and again and again He referred to the Old Testament Scriptures as an infallible and unbreakable source of truth.

> Matthew 21:42 *Have you never read in the Scriptures...*

> Matthew 22:29 *You are in error because you do not know the Scriptures...*

> Matthew 26:54 *How then would the Scriptures be fulfilled...*

> Luke 4:21 *Today this Scripture is fulfilled in your hearing...*

> Luke 24:44 *Everything must be fulfilled that is written about Me in the Law of Moses, the Prophets and the Psalms.*

> Luke 24:45 *Then He opened their minds so, they could understand the Scriptures...*

> John 7:38 *Whoever believes in Me, as Scripture has said...*

> John 7:42 *Does not the Scripture say...*

He summed it up by saying,

> *... Scripture cannot be set aside.* John 10:35

The apostle Paul confirms that, although men's hands wrote the actual words,[173] all Scripture is God–breathed.[174]

You cannot, repeat *cannot*, believe the Old Testament accounts have been severely disproved by the wisdom of this world and still keep Jesus—*as revealed in Scripture*—separated out as an intact, isolated, unsullied item of belief.

Just as you cannot separate Moses from the New Testament, you cannot separate Jesus from the Old Testament.

Derek Prince wrote, 'If we believe in Jesus then we believe in the Bible. If we do not believe in the Bible then we do not believe in Jesus.'[175]

A very large number of people, including many leaders, have decided there is a heaven but no hell. It is but a dark age myth. And so concern for the hell–bound world has almost disappeared from the Christian's heart and mind.

Yet Jesus affirmed its reality again and again and again.[176] (More about this in chapter 13.)

A large number of people, including many leaders, have decided there are, or may be, other ways to get to heaven outside of personal faith in Jesus and His finished work on the cross.[177] Yet Jesus made it clear that "no one comes to the Father except through Me".[178] This clear doctrine—that for centuries has sent missionaries to the four corners of the earth—is underlined in the book of Acts where it is written,

> Jesus is the Word become flesh, not a mixture of myth and The Word that became flesh.

> *"Salvation is found in no one else, for there is no other name under heaven given to mankind by which we must be saved."* Acts 4:12

These large numbers of people, including many leaders, are thus declaring Jesus and the apostles were naïve to believe and proclaim such a thing. They were but "men of their day, with the understanding of their day".

Thus—irrespective of how nicely it is dressed up—for them, Jesus cannot be 'The Truth.' And if not 'The Truth' then He cannot be 'The Way' and 'The Life'.[179]

Jesus is the Word become flesh, not a mixture of myth and The Word that became flesh. He is The Truth, not a mixture of myth and The Truth. God makes it clear again and again that *He will not have mixtures.* (Leviticus 19:19, Deuteronomy 22:9, 2 Corinthians 6:14–16) It is therefore safe to say that He has not permitted His Word to be a mixture.

> *"Every word of God is flawless; He is a shield to those who take refuge in Him. Do not add to His words, or He will rebuke you and prove you a liar..."* Proverbs 30:5–6

However taking away from God's Word brings more than a rebuke. On the last few sentences on the last page of the last book in the Bible we read a dire warning. If it is applicable to this last, prophetic, book of the Bible, surely it must be applicable to the very core of Scripture itself.

> *...And if anyone takes words away from this scroll of prophecy, God will take away from that person any share in the tree of life and in the Holy City, which are described in this scroll.* Revelation 22:19

Throughout the ages past, and in many countries in this present age, hundreds of thousands of people have chosen to go to their death rather than add, take away from or deny the integrity of Scripture. They understood. What this host of witnesses must think of our many underlying layers of unbelief I can only imagine.

The 'god of this world', 'the ruler of this world', that old serpent called Satan could not get the old saints to deny one line of Scripture—even while being burnt at the stake. Yet today, as 'the prince of the power of the air' he can get millions to ditch huge chunks of doctrine through a television documentary or a popular hyped–up book written by an atheist.

From page one onwards the acts of God are supernatural. They are, and always will be, foolishness to the wise of this world. Foolishness to the natural man.[180] The natural man says that these things cannot be done—therefore they were not done. The parting of the Red Sea cannot be done. The floating of an iron axe-head cannot be done. Walking on water cannot be done. Water turning instantly to wine cannot be done. Feeding thousands on one boy's small lunch cannot be done. The raising of the dead cannot be done.

But they were done.

The miracle of the new birth is supernatural and the natural man cannot comprehend it.

When natural men succeed in getting us to view the supernatural acts of God in Scripture through their unopened eyes and their natural understanding, then we join them in their darkness. The Bible—rather than revealing truth—closes over.

If you struggle with any of these issues, then the best prayer is that of the distressed child's father as recorded in Mark 9:24 NKJV—

"Lord, I believe; help my unbelief."

But to continue to hold a view contrary to what Jesus directly, or indirectly, affirmed as truth, puts you in great disagreement with the God you claim to worship.

That prince of preachers Charles Haddon Spurgeon said, "If I did not believe in the infallibility of Scripture—the absolute infallibility of it from cover to cover, I would never enter this pulpit again!"

The epistles have much to say about those who do not abide in sound doctrine. The doctrine that Christ's appointed apostles taught, wrote about and usually died for. The doctrine that has been passed down to us—often at great cost—throughout the generations.

All Christians know, or should know, that the Holy Spirit will only witness that which can be confirmed through Scripture. It used to be that Scripture judged us. Now, under great pressure from the world, we have been trained to judge Scripture. When it is 'thus saith the Lord' versus 'thus saith the world', all too often we immediately bow the knee to the latter.

When we are trained to think like the 'natural man', the next layer of questioning will inevitably be the virgin birth and then the resurrection. After all, observable science can prove a woman cannot become pregnant without physical semen from a man, and can prove someone severely beaten, crucified, speared in the heart, pronounced dead and then entombed for three days cannot just get up and walk away. And then ascend into heaven! After all, our only 'proof' is that it says so in Scripture.

> Deceiving spirits bring discord and disunity by propagating the age old question that brought about Adam's fall, "Did God really say...?"

If we have stopped thinking in 'supernatural' terms to explain the earlier recorded events in Scripture, how then can we justify adopting that stance now?

Have I gone too far?

Brian Edwards (former President of the *Fellowship of Independent Evangelical Churches*) in his excellent book *Nothing But The Truth*[181] states that around one–third of Anglican Bishops do not believe in the virgin birth or the resurrection. Indeed I remember a previous Bishop of Durham claim the resurrection of Christ was "merely a conjuring trick with bones"[182] and I recently heard a Bishop on television stating that his faith did not rest on the virgin birth. (If Jesus had an earthly father like us, then, like us, He would have been the offspring of Adam, and like us, would have needed a heaven–sent Saviour.[183])

If the Holy Spirit is not persuading men and women to distance themselves from teachings that Jesus affirmed directly or indirectly, then which spirits might be at work?

These can only be deceiving spirits, and these spirits have indeed caused great splits in the church. Their success can be judged by the painful reality that many teachers who hold to the traditional authority of Scripture from beginning to end will rarely get a church pulpit or a Bible seminary post. Some have even been heckled in church. (Ask those who work for Creation Ministries.)

A Barna survey showed that less than one out of every five *born again Christians* (USA sample) have even a basic Biblical worldview.[184] It must be assumed that the survey respondents either attend, or have attended church, and listened to teaching. No wonder teachers will be judged more strictly![185]

The Holy Spirit brings unity around His Word. That unity brings a great anointing.[186] Deceiving spirits bring discord and disunity by propagating the age old question that brought about Adam's fall, "Did God really say...?"[187] The fourth chapter of Paul's first letter to Timothy is usually given the heading, *The Great Apostasy*, where the first verse reads...

> *The Spirit clearly says that in later times some will abandon the faith and follow deceiving spirits and things taught by demons...*

Satan is the Goliath who relentlessly taunts the people of God. Sometimes it seems that we, God's people, are standing huddled together on the hillside, trembling with fear and weakness as 'the god of this world' daily paces up and down before us, mocking us for our beliefs through his many articulate spokesmen.

In David's day Scripture was comprised of five books called *The Torah*— Genesis, Exodus, Leviticus, Numbers and Deuteronomy. David picked five stones out of the river. I believe these stones represented the written word of God as it existed then. He struck down the mocking giant with the very first stone. And suddenly the church of the day was empowered.

David was what they were not. A man after God's own heart.

I believe the first stone David killed the taunting giant with represented the first book. Genesis. That stone is now being thrown back at the church and we are being knocked down and the enemy empowered. God's Word is the sword of the Spirit.[188] Satan, tempting Jesus during His forty days of testing in the wilderness, could not—even once—get past Jesus' authoritative declaration, "*It is written.*"[189]

The mocking was silenced.

When those who claim Jesus as their Lord and God reject the integrity of God's Word, they become spiritually powerless. Like Samson, the seven locks of their hair are being cut one by one, and their spiritual eyesight is dimming towards blindness.[190] They can no longer, with integrity of faith, and thus authority, boldly say, "It is written."

Knowing that he was close to death, and speaking of doctrine, Paul was able to say,

> *For I am already being poured out like a drink offering, and the time for my departure is near. I have fought the good fight, I have finished the race,* ***I have kept the faith.*** 2 Timothy 4:6–7 [emphasis mine]

Let Paul's triumphant declaration be ours as well.

"Did God really say?"

Yes He did!

Some probing questions:

- Do you believe that this chapter is in line with Scripture?

- Are there areas in your belief that are contrary to what Jesus affirms?

- What is your reaction to this chapter?

- If you were in a serious situation and wanted prayer, would you choose a man or woman who believed in the complete integrity of Scripture or a person who believed that many parts of Scripture were unreliable? Or would that make no difference to you?

SEVEN
Which Side of the Cross?

The last chapter was all about the belt of truth. Not your belt of truth, not the world's belt of truth, but God's belt of truth.[191] The "it is written" word of God.[192] The sword of the Spirit.[193]

There is a war on and you're involved whether you want to be or not.[194]

It's a war between two opposing kingdoms and in order to be able to move on with God you need to be aware of, and alert to, this tension.[195] You need to know your authority,[196] your weapons[197] and of course you must know your opponent's tactics.[198]

Truth sets you free.[199] Truth sets others free. Lies open you to deception, which in turn opens you to bondage.[200] The shield of faith is active trust that what God says is true and that He watches over His word to perform it.[201] Just knowing what truth is does not give you authority. Submitting to truth and obeying the One who is Truth does.[202]

Ask the sons of Sceva. They knew the words that the apostle Paul used to such effect. However, Satan knew they were not obedient believers operating under divine authority and he easily harassed them.

> *God did extraordinary miracles through Paul, so that even handkerchiefs and aprons that had touched him were taken to the*

*sick, and their illnesses were cured and the evil spirits left them. Some Jews who went around driving out evil spirits tried to invoke the name of the Lord Jesus over those who were demon–possessed. They would say, "In the name of the Jesus whom Paul preaches, I command you to come out." Seven sons of Sceva, a Jewish chief priest, were doing this. One day the evil spirit answered them, "**Jesus I know, and Paul I know about, but who are you?**" Then the man who had the evil spirit jumped on them and overpowered them all. He gave them such a beating that they ran out of the house naked and bleeding.* Acts 19:11–16 [emphasis mine]

Satan's tactics are simple but deadly to the unwary or unknowledgeable Christian.

He sows doubt in what God declares to be truth,[203] he deceives,[204] he tempts,[205] he accuses[206] he torments,[207] and he suggests you are a Christian with no authority.[208]

This is where we pick up on the title of this chapter.

We all have a history and Satan will seek to discourage you by continually bringing various ungodly events to your remembrance. These events are behind the cross. Yes, they happened, but they are behind the cross. Forgiven.

> We are called to live
>
> 'behind' the cross...
>
> to deal with sin issues
>
> immediately...
>
> This is called the
>
> repentant lifestyle.

Finished to God's satisfaction.[209] (Though consequences and unhealed wounds from the past may need healing; but more about that in chapter 9.)

But listen also to this. If you are choosing to live sinfully then these deliberate sins are on the wrong side of the cross and open to satanic attack. They might not affect your salvation but they most certainly will affect your life. They will also stop you from moving on with God.

I have met people who are at ease with their sin. They claim their wilful behavior is under and therefore automatically cleansed by the Blood! Not so. They are confusing their legal position under grace with their experiential walk. Charles Haddon Spurgeon said, "Grace is the mother and nurse of holiness, and not the apologist of sin."[210]

If we are walking in the Light, then the blood of Jesus purifies us. Not when we deliberately choose to walk in darkness.

> *If we claim to have fellowship with Him and yet walk in the darkness, we lie and do not live out the truth. But if we walk in the light, as He is in the light, we have fellowship with one another, and the blood of Jesus, His Son, purifies us from all sin.* 1 John 1:6–7

We have been transferred from the dominion of darkness into the Kingdom of God's Son through the forgiveness of our sins[211] and as such we are called to live 'behind' the cross. To walk carefully.[212] To examine ourselves[213] and to deal with sin issues immediately and make sure they are quickly repented of, and 'dead'. This is called the repentant lifestyle.[214] The apostle Paul advises us to deal with sin issues before the day's end lest the devil get a foothold.

> *"In your anger do not sin." Do not let the sun go down while you are still angry, and do not give the devil a foothold.* Ephesians 4:26–27

This lifestyle helps us to remain 'filled with the Spirit'[215] but if we don't choose that lifestyle we can grieve the Holy Spirit,[216] and risk quenching the Holy Spirit.[217]

Every weed begins with a seed and, though an ungodly thought may seem harmless, it is a seed which, if quietly accepted and nourished, will take root and eventually become an action. This simple illustration shows the journey from freedom into bondage to sin, with the demonic seeking to get a foothold at stage two, then gradually building a stronghold. Which means it has gained a strong hold in your life!

Stage one –>	Stage two –>	Stage three –>	Stage four –>
Ungodly thought	Ungodly action	Ungodly habit	Stronghold

When something is stronger than our will to resist it, then we have a stronghold within. Knowing we are in a war, our safeguard is to train ourselves to take every thought captive because every ungodly *action* begins with an ungodly *thought*. Every lust begins with an ungodly imagining that is given room to grow.

> *We demolish arguments and every pretension that sets itself up against the knowledge of God, and we take captive every thought to make it obedient to Christ.* 2 Corinthians 10:5

Many Christians lead lives that are daily lived on the wrong side of the cross. They will never be able to move on with God while they live there. I confess I am often dismayed by the amount of deliberate, wilful sin within the Body of Christ. Shocking! Shocking! *Shocking!* There I've said it. Shocking because it shouldn't be.

> *Have nothing to do with the fruitless deeds of darkness, but rather expose them. It is shameful even to mention what the disobedient do in secret.* Ephesians 5:11–12

Little sins un–repented grow into big sins, yet so often we are deceived into seeing no danger in 'little sins'. But like 'little foxes, they do ruin the vineyard.'[218] Eventually.

They give the enemy rights and he will draw near and lock on to them in order to steal, kill and destroy.[219] God can only bless what He can bless, and so our deliberate unrepentant sinful behavior will cause Him to withdraw His hand with the result we lose our battles.[220] The Old Testament so often gives us a physical picture to help us understand the spiritual. Let me quote this graphic portion of Scripture including the translators' sub–heading.

Uncleanness in the Camp

> *When you are encamped against your enemies, keep away from everything impure. If one of your men is unclean because of a nocturnal emission, he is to go outside the camp and stay there. But as evening approaches he is to wash himself, and at sunset he may return to the camp. Designate a place outside the camp where you can go to relieve yourself. As part of your equipment have something to dig with, and*

when you relieve yourself, dig a hole and cover up your excrement. **For the Lord your God moves about in your camp to protect you and to deliver your enemies to you. Your camp must be holy, so that He will not see among you anything indecent and turn away from you.** Deuteronomy 23:9–14 [emphasis mine]

Another physical picture from the Old Testament is when Achan's hidden sin gave the Canaanite village of Ai an easy victory over the armies of Israel. Victory only came when the sin was dealt with.[221] Un–removed dog poo attracts flies just as un–dealt with sin attracts the demonic. Un–dealt with anger will attract spirits of anger. Lust will attract spirits of lust. And so on. You can live one of two ways. You can spend your life swatting flies or you can remove the dog poo.

When we are born again, we are new creations with a brand new nature. We know the Scripture well.

> *Therefore, if anyone is in Christ, the new creation has come: The old has gone, the new is here!* 2 Corinthians 5:17

We should be just as aware of the verses that follow later in the same letter, especially this one:

> *Therefore, since we have these promises, dear friends, let us purify ourselves from everything that contaminates body and spirit, perfecting holiness out of reverence for God.* 2 Corinthians 7:1

We all sin. No point is saying that we don't. Even the most obedient heart can mess up. Genuine repentance[222] puts the mess–up behind the cross and removes Satan's claim.

> *If we claim to be without sin, we deceive ourselves and the truth is not in us. If we confess our sins, he is faithful and just and will forgive us our sins and purify us from all unrighteousness.* 1 John 1:8–9

Thus, old sin, genuinely repented, lies dead behind the cross.[223]

New sin, lived in and un–repented, stands alive and well on the wrong side of the cross. On the side where Satan has full access and legal right. While you live there, carelessly, you will never move on with God.

Which side of the cross do you live on?

Some probing questions:

- Is there a sin you have 'made friends with'?

- Are there any sins safely behind the cross that Satan torments you with?

EIGHT
A Divided Life?

In order to move on with God we need to check our Kingdom mindset is correct, otherwise we can miss out on much blessing. This is an example of what I mean.

Many of us think and speak of our church building or Christian centre as God's house. *"I am going to God's house on Sunday"* and *"Welcome to God's house, sir."* And of course, in a very real sense it is. It is a building set apart and dedicated to God's plans and purposes and should be treated with due reverence. It is a property used for teaching, preaching, prayer, worship and fellowship. It is a place we trust will be powerfully used by God. However, although it is thus rightly spoken of as 'God's House', God does not *live* there and a wrong understanding of this much–used phrase can lead to a divided life.

God is omnipresent (everywhere) inhabiting even the highest heaven,[224] yet in the Old Testament, God chose to tabernacle (to live) in the midst of His people. He did this by 'dwelling' first in a moveable tent,[225] and then in an immoveable temple. His earthly dwelling place was of course, always a sacred place. A very sacred place. The most sacred place on earth!

A place so sacred only one man, the High Priest, bearing the blood of an innocent animal, was allowed to enter the very inner sanctum—the

> When that man–made
> 'trinity' was dedicated
> to God, His Presence
> was pleased to come
> and dwell within it.

most holy place—once a year.[226] It is understood a rope was tied around his ankles in case he was struck dead as he entered into the Presence of God through the heavy curtain where the Ark of the Covenant resided. If the bells around the hem of his garment fell silent and there was no response from him, the watchers would know both he and the sacrificial blood he had presented on their behalf had been rejected. They would then be able to pull him out of the Most Holy Place by the rope. When the people saw that their High Priest had been accepted they knew that they too were accepted.[227] As equally accepted as the High Priest inside! That's a powerful image to attach to 'God's dwelling place'.

All this was the 'type' for the New Testament spiritual. Take Solomon's temple for instance:

- The outside wall was stone taken from the earth.[228] (Flesh)

- The stone was then completely covered on the inside with cedar wood.[229] (Soul)

- Finally the cedar wood was covered on the inside with Gold.[230] (Spirit)

When that man–made 'trinity' was dedicated to God, His Presence was pleased to come and dwell within it. And so, that place was God's *visible* temple on earth. His *visible* dwelling Place.[231] His house. And what a precious place for Him to dwell in! However, Calvary changed everything! When Jesus died on the cross, the heavy Temple curtain separating the Holy Place from the Most Holy Place was dramatically torn from top to bottom.[232] From heaven to earth. Powerfully signifying that God's vital Presence was no longer confined there.[233] A huge New Testament truth to be proclaimed is that God does not live in temples made with hands.

*The God who made the world and everything in it is Lord of heaven and earth and **does not live in temples built by human hands**.* Acts 17:24 [emphasis mine]

The Old Testament's tent, temple and rituals were the promise of the real that was to come.[234] The real—in every sense—was *Jesus*.[235] When He, the Lamb of God, entered God's Presence as our Great High Priest, offering His own blood, He was fully accepted, which means that we, whom He represents, are accepted also![236] *As equally accepted as our Great High Priest!* What a powerful truth. Amazing grace! We now meet God *in*,[237] and *through* Jesus Christ.[238] Jesus spoke of His body as 'this temple'[239] in whom the apostle Paul wrote, 'dwells all the fullness of the Godhead bodily.'[240] Little wonder that the term *'in Christ'* is used so often throughout the New Testament.[241] But here is the point of this chapter. When we were born again, God's Spirit, 'the Spirit of Christ',[242] the Holy Spirit came to live in us. You and I are now His Holy temple!

He breathed on them, and said to them, "Receive the Holy Spirit." John 20:22

The apostle Paul wrote to the church at Corinth to proclaim this great truth.

*...**you** are the temple of the living God. As God has said: "I will dwell in them and walk among them. I will be their God, and they shall be My people."* 2 Corinthians 6:16 [emphasis mine]

Pause and consider the unimaginable value He puts on us in whom His Spirit dwells. You and I, individually and corporately, are now His *visible* temple on earth.[243] And here is the lesson; that temple is sacred. Very sacred! The most sacred place on earth!

*Don't you know that you yourselves are God's temple and that God's Spirit dwells in your midst? If anyone destroys God's temple, God will destroy that person; for God's temple is sacred, and **you together are that temple**.* 1 Corinthians 3:16–17 [emphasis mine]

No wonder the apostle John could proclaim,

> Unbelievers see the hypocrisy in behaving righteously in church on Sunday and living another way the rest of the week.

...the one who is in you is greater than the one who is in the world. 1 John 4:4 [emphasis mine]

When we think of the word 'church' we have become accustomed to think of a man–made building used for religious services. Indeed, Webster's dictionary has this as the primary meaning of the word. In the New Testament however, the word church— *ekklesia*—could be more accurately translated as "assembly" or "congregation". Anywhere we sincerely[244] gather together in Jesus' Name is where God in Christ is pleased to manifest Himself and dwell.

> *For where two or three come together in My name, there am I with them.* Matthew 18:20

That meeting place could be a church building, a house, a jail, a beach, a rooftop, a cathedral, a gospel hall, a mud hut, a tent, a rented hotel room or a mountainside.

You get the point I'm sure, *but is it an important point?*

I believe it is.

Many of us live our lives as if they were divided into the sacred and non–sacred. It is predominantly a western mindset. For instance, a man might speak graciously to his wife in a certain way because on Sunday they are in 'God's House'. Then the moment he exits the door he might feel free to talk to her in a less honouring way because they are now outside God's House. A woman might not indulge in gossip while in Church because she is in 'God's House'. Yet on returning to life outside she might give free rein to this behavior because she believes she is no longer in God's immediate Presence. He lives 'in Church'—in a building.

Unbelievers see the hypocrisy in behaving righteously in church on Sunday and living another way the rest of the week. And they are influenced away from Jesus. Mahatma Ghandi was turned away from Christianity and remained Hindu. He said, "I don't reject your Christ. I love your Christ. It's just that so many of you Christians are so unlike your Christ."

He also claimed that, "If Christians would really live according to the teachings of Christ, as found in the Bible, all of India would be Christian today."

French philosopher and writer Voltaire said, "If Christians want us to believe in a Redeemer, let them act redeemed."

The Jewish people have always understood that *every part* of their existence is sacred. Even going to the toilet.

> "Blessed be the Lord God, King of the Universe, who has created humans with wisdom, with openings and hollow parts, revealed before your holy throne, that if any part of the body was to malfunction, it would be impossible for us to exist and stand before you for even a short time. You cure all flesh and perform wonders."

In the Old Testament, priests were people especially set apart by God to minister to God and to the people. Their positions were indeed sacred. However, even under the New Covenant, we still tend to view the pastor/minister who holds Kingdom office as 'sacred' and we the laity as not. Too often the perception is that we don't have to live our lives unto God as holy as they do. But we do![245] We are all priests unto God, all part of God's sacred spiritual house, as the apostle Peter emphasized.

> *...you also, as living stones, are being built up a spiritual house, a holy priesthood, to offer up spiritual sacrifices acceptable to God through Jesus Christ.* 1 Peter 2:5 [emphasis mine]

> *But you are a chosen generation, a royal priesthood, a holy nation, His own special people, that you may proclaim the praises of Him*

> If we develop a faulty Kingdom mind–set we can hinder our development as Christians.

who called you out of darkness into His marvellous light. 1 Peter 2:9 [emphasis mine]

We would be horrified (rightly) if at church a large screen television was set up and certain unsavoury television programs or movies were played. Because we define the church building alone as being sacred. Yet (wrongly) in our homes, we cross these boundaries continually because we do not classify our home as sacred.

Missionaries are (rightly) regarded as sacred and are prayed for at the front of the church. Yet (wrongly) the men and women who go into the mission field of secular work daily, praying that they might be light in darkness[246] would never expect the same sort of prayer. Because we classify missionaries as sacred and ourselves as not. Leaders deserve honour, of course—even double honour[247]—but they are not in the sacred camp, while we are standing outside looking in!

Our tithe is (rightly) regarded as sacred, but (wrongly) the rest is usually not regarded as such. Our ministry or church work is (rightly) regarded as sacred, but (wrongly) our business, our marriage and especially the marriage bed are usually not thought of as sacred.

Quiet times at home are (rightly) regarded as sacred. But (wrongly) as soon as we move into the day we revert back to *au naturel.* Because the rest of the day is usually not regarded as sacred.

Can you see? If we develop a faulty Kingdom mind–set we can hinder our development as Christians. Once we confine God's interaction with our lives into the sacred and the non–sacred then, starting with our church building, we fall into the trap of dual thinking and dual behavior: the 'Sunday saint' and the 'Monday sinner'. Consequently a portion of our lives and behavior is set apart for God and the rest is set aside for ourselves.

What does an undivided life look like? Nineteen years ago I wrote this short plea to Jesus from the depth of my heart. I still remember the evening that I wrote it. I had just come back from a training run on a cold wet evening. I went upstairs to the bedroom, closed the door, wrote it out and then put it into the *Good News Bible* my mother had bought for Linda and I when she heard we had become Christians.

> Here's the big idea. In God's eyes every part of our life is sacred.

It's on a small piece of paper, folded neatly in half, and it still resides in the same Bible. The opening line is on the outside cover.

Dear Jesus, I want…

The main content is in the inside portion,

> *…to give more of me to You; to trust You more than me; to praise You with actions; to see You in every person less fortunate than me; to think first what You would say before I speak; to think first what You would do before I do; to fully understand Your will for me; to love more; to encourage more; to heal more; to confess You more; to be more humble; to be more joyful; to be more peaceful; to live in You; to die in You; to meet You:*

…with the concluding sentence on the back cover,

Dear Jesus, please give me what I want.

Am I there yet? If only! But the desire for Jesus to be glorified in every part of my life, every moment of every day still burns within me.

Here's the big idea. In God's eyes every part of our life is sacred. All day. Every day. How beautiful. How precious. When we understand and agree with that, things change!

> *But just as He who called you is holy, so **be holy in all you do**.* 1 Peter 1:15 [emphasis mine]

May we be true ambassadors for Christ. Always. Everywhere. Our heart, His home.

Some probing questions:

- What have you classified as sacred and non–sacred in your life?

- How has this affected your thinking and behavior?

NINE
Simon's Story

A very troubled Christian with a very troubled past said to me, "I'm born again, a new creation, so I don't live in the past." To which I replied, "Indeed, but some of the consequences from your past still live in you." And a light went on.

The long generational line we have emerged from, the parenting and the home life we were raised in, the culture of the country and the era we are living in, our status, our wealth or poverty, the births, the marriages and the deaths, the great friendships and the terrible fallouts, the joys and the sadness in our lives—plus many other factors—have all played a part in shaping us. Some things left good consequences, others not so good.

In order to really move on with God it is helpful—in some cases essential—to deal with some of the negative consequences from the past. Pushing things down or pretending they don't exist doesn't work for long. The prodigal came home to the father and the father instantly put the best robe around him and celebrated his homecoming. The son was forgiven and safely home. The ring on the finger and the sandals on the feet showed he was a full member of the family. A joint heir with the other son.[248] The old rebellious life was gone. All things were new from now on. But underneath the cloak the consequences and wounds from past events would have left their mark and would have needed healing. And that would be a process.

> Despite our theology being correct on one level, damaging past experiences can still dictate much of our mindset, heart beliefs and behavior.

We all know what Jesus was picturing for us. When we came home to the Father through Jesus, our rebellion over, the Father joyfully robed us with the best robe and the righteousness of Christ.[249] Heaven celebrated.[250] All things were new. Our names were written in the family Book of Life[251] and we were declared to be joint–heirs with God's only begotten Son.[252]

Yet, underneath this invisible but very real spiritual robe of Christ's righteousness, past events have left their mark. We may need healing. Despite our theology being correct on one level, damaging past experiences can still dictate much of our mindset, heart beliefs and behavior.[253] For instance, we know our worth in Christ, yet deep within us we can still operate out of low self–worth coming from early years of rejection. Left unchecked this can develop into self–rejection. ("It must be me.") Then comes a gradual withdrawal from community due to the fear of suffering further rejection. Finally isolation, loneliness, hopelessness and despair can set in. Wrong direction! About turn! So often what people have been praying into, or had prayer for, are the symptoms (picture the leaves of a weed) rather than dealing with the root buried somewhere down in our timeline. Like cutting a lawn, all looks well on the surface for a week or two. Then the hidden roots of the weeds reproduce the leaves. The problem is back. Maybe a bit of thought will reveal the root cause because it's obvious. Maybe you need a brilliant Counsellor, Helper and Comforter to reveal it. May I recommend the Holy Spirit? These are just some of His precious offices towards us. If you struggle with that, ask Jesus to lead you to an experienced prayer ministry team, mature Christian counsellors or a Christian ministry that runs courses dealing with most issues.[254] Twenty years of teaching and prayer ministry service has certainly shown me that a substantial, and ever–increasing proportion of the Body of Christ, need healing and even deliverance—the bread of the children[255]—from the consequences of past events.

Let me tell you Simon's story.

I first saw Simon way back in the late 90s. I was the speaker at a Wednesday evening meeting held for people too fragile in spirit and soul to attend the big Sunday services. I was sitting with the elder who had invited me and, as the people began arriving, I sensed the Lord fixing my eyes on a well–built man in his early thirties. I felt the Lord witnessing to my spirit that, before I spoke, I was to tell this man that there was a call on his life. And this I did. After being introduced by the elder I stood up and pointed to this man who was seated along the back wall of the room, and asked him to stand up. He was clearly uncomfortable with this sudden spotlight, so I kept the word as brief as I could. I meant to say, "The Lord has asked me to tell you that there is a call on your life," but I am told I actually said, "Don't despair, the Lord has asked me to tell you that there is a call on your life." He sat down and I carried on with the rest of the evening. However at the end of the evening the elder in charge asked me if I really thought that word had been from God. "Yes," I said. "Otherwise I would never have given it. Why do you ask that?" And then I heard about Simon's history. Simon joined the Royal Navy in 1984 and was promoted as a navigating officer, also specializing as a pilot. While on a three–week survival training exercise in the New Forest, in temperatures of 90 degrees he developed heatstroke and septicaemia, and began to behave in a disorientated manner. Eventually he collapsed. What happened next is hard to believe, but the training officer began to physically and verbally assault him. A couple walking their dog in the New Forest came upon the scene and twice intervened, probably saving Simon's life. The man told the court of enquiry that he saw Simon being hauled to his feet, being punched on the back of the neck, being hauled up by his hair and being verbally abused.[256] Simon went into a coma, his brain massively swollen. An ambulance was called and he was rushed into hospital where he remained in the coma for twenty days. The hospital said that a weaker man would almost certainly have died. When he came out of the coma he was seriously brain–damaged and, after one year mostly spent in the naval and tri–services hospitals, he was released from the armed forces on medical grounds, and entered the National Health Service facilities. He was married with a very young daughter and it seemed as though all their lives were as good as over.

Simon's wife was originally from Northern Ireland so she decided to bring Simon and their daughter back there. The following years were quite horrific due to Simon's behavior. It ranged from silent and sullen to frighteningly aggressive, and at times when he escaped from his wife Julie's care, he would drink himself into a coma. After years of this behavior someone invited him to a Christian meeting and he gave his life to Jesus, hence his presence at this meeting some weeks later. He was still severely brain–damaged and his speech was almost incoherent. I confess that when I heard this story I began to doubt I had indeed heard from God. How could God use such a damaged human being? Simon later said that from that evening his behavior and his despair actually got worse and he made several unsuccessful suicide attempts.

Years went by. One day I borrowed a new–fangled power hose to clean the steps at the front of my house. Outside the front door were three large paving stones, and then six paving stone steps leading down to the driveway. In my mind the power hose would clean the green algae from the paving stones within a half hour. To my dismay after a half hour only the three paving stones at the front door were clean. This, of course, showed up the remaining pavers in an even worse light. However, by this stage I was cold, wet and bored and decided to do the steps another day. Still, to ensure I would not 'forget' to finish the job, in a moment of inspiration/ madness I used the power hose to write my name KEN on the first step. Then on the next step, in script I wrote LINDA. Then on the remaining steps I wrote each of our children's names in descending order of birth. When I finished I was quite pleased with the result. Not so Linda! When she came back from shopping she thought it looked awful. So I promised I would finish the cleaning the following day. Next morning I was in my home–office at the front of the house when, through the window, I noticed a lady who was obviously looking for a particular house. I recognized her as a member of the church I had previously belonged to, and was pleasantly surprised when she decided our house was the one she wanted. She quickly made her way up the steps past my office window. I opened the front door and she immediately asked if I remembered a 'word' I had had for a young man many years ago at the church she attended. I said that I did.

"How can you remember so far back?" she asked. That was easy! "It's the only time it's happened to me!" I replied.

She said the young man was in the mental unit of a nearby hospital, suffering from terrifying flashbacks that compelled him to escape from the hospital. He had been found crawling around the grounds on his elbows with mud smeared on his face as though he were back on the survival course. She said he had suddenly asked if they could find the man who, many years ago, had told him there was a call on his life. No one knew where I lived, but someone knew the general proximity. So she'd come and, as she was looking around, she saw the steps outside our home with the family names on them!

I agreed to go and see Simon that evening. When I arrived at the hospital car park I met Julie, his wife. She told me Simon had just cut his wrists so it would be a while before we were allowed in. That shocked me. Sure enough, half an hour later we were admitted into the ward, and there, behind closed curtains I met Simon again. His wrists were bandaged and he sat sideways to me on the edge of the bed, between Julie and me, just staring at the curtain in front of him.

I explained to him that, as a Christian, he was called to forgive the man responsible, but I took the time to explain what that meant. Simon said afterwards many people had told him he had to forgive, but until that moment, he had not understood why or what it entailed. He thought about it, then nodded his head in agreement. I led him slowly in a prayer of forgiveness, which was sincerely meant, but barely coherent.

His wife Julie was speechless. (Rare—by her own admission!) On one hand she saw an amazing change in her husband's eyes—'life' she called it—but on the other hand she was not a Christian and could not believe what her suffering husband had just done. Forgiven that man! How could he?

But Simon had indeed forgiven and this opened the way to an amazing journey of restoration. I went back the following evening and met Julie in the car park, where I was told that Simon had now cut his stomach with a broken cup. Again, shocked, we waited for half an hour before gaining entry to the unit.

There, seated again on the edge of his bed and staring at the curtain, was Simon. He was bare–chested, his midriff well–bandaged. A blood–stained white tee–shirt was rolled up at the end of the bed.

I slowly explained to him that, on the previous evening, he had forgiven the instructor,[257] but now it was right to cut all ungodly ties between them. I explained that God designed us all to be able to bond so we could be a blessing to others, but when two lives had been bonded by distress it was important to ask Jesus to separate that unseen but very real tie. He nodded in agreement and I prayed accordingly. That proved to be the last time Simon attacked himself.

Some time later I asked if Simon could come out for the afternoon. The unit agreed, and slowly we got to know each other better. Then the unit asked Julie if Simon could be tried at home again for a night. She agreed but, at midnight, I got an anxious call from her saying Simon was sitting in sullen silence at the kitchen table simmering with a pent–up explosive rage and they were very frightened. I came round immediately and will never forget the sight of Simon—a big man—sitting at the end of the kitchen staring straight ahead of him. His fists were on the table top tightly clenched.

I approached rather cautiously and sat down next to him. As I spoke, he never once looked at me but continued to stare straight ahead. I explained to him that because of the violence he had suffered and the anger he had kept so pent up there was a strong possibility the demonic would have latched on to that brokenness. I asked if he would be agreeable to me praying accordingly. After a minute he nodded slightly so I prayed in that understanding.

That ended that phase. Events continued in this fashion. Over the next eighteen months or so, Simon was gradually set free from a great variety of issues. His sense of balance had been so damaged he always needed to see horizontals and verticals otherwise he would fall down. On a trip with me to a men's conference I was speaking at in Scotland, God healed him of this problem without anyone praying for him. He had a fear of snakes—he has no idea why—and would check under the bed at night before getting into it. God set him free from that.

His brain healed and so did his speech. There is still just enough of a difficulty to be a reminder of his past. When Simon gives his testimony he always says the next part was God's biggest miracle of all. His daughter Ruth had grown up terrified, not only of her father (for obvious reasons) but of all men. Even though God was healing and restoring her father, she could not develop any sense of security. It was so bad that, if he came into a room, she would run out. She would not agree to be left alone with him. She clung to her mum like a limpet.

One afternoon he phoned me and said he couldn't stand the pain of this anymore so I asked him to come to my house to pray. I can't remember what we prayed, but Jesus can. Simon drove home, some ten minutes away and, as he parked the car in the driveway, the door opened and Ruth ran out into his arms crying and saying she loved him. To this day it would be hard to find a closer pair in this world! (Remembering this always gets Simon teary–eyed!)

A year or so later God put it on my heart that Simon was to be a member of our close–knit ministry team. I waited another year to be certain I had definitely heard from God. But I had. Simon has not only been on the team for more than a decade, he is one of the best prayer ministry members of the team. He's also growing into an accomplished speaker.

Along the way Julie wholeheartedly gave her life to Jesus. She needed much emotional healing as a consequence of the years of trauma and despair. She also required healing from her somewhat belligerent attitude, entirely due to years of fighting aggressively on Simon's behalf.

> When Christians walk clean before God, it affects the present and the future.

But the miracles kept coming and God has done a great work in her life also. So much so that not only is she now a member of our team, but she has one of the gentlest, most God–sensitive hearts on the team. To hear Julie pray is to know that many of the things that break God's heart also breaks hers! Their daughter Ruth has become one of the finest young Christian ladies you could ever meet, and she is now training to be a doctor. "Sir, God has a call on your life." Indeed He did. Indeed He has.

Admittedly this is an extreme case, but I hope the point is made. When a person truly repents, it affects the future. When Christians walk clean before God, it affects the present and the future. Healing and deliverance deals with the past, and issuing forgiveness to those responsible for any spiritual, emotional, physiological, financial or physical wounding is definitely one of the major keys in that process. God really wants His people to live in liberty. In Ezekiel chapter 34 we read of God's righteous anger when the shepherds of His people will not care for or bind up the wounds of His people.

> *You have not strengthened the weak or healed the sick or bound up the injured.* Ezekiel 34:4

He then declares that He will be that Shepherd.

> *...I will bind up the injured and strengthen the weak...* Ezekiel 34:16

Some six hundred years later, in the New Testament, we are introduced to Jesus, 'Immanuel', *God with us*,[258] as the Great Shepherd.[259] In the synagogue He stands up, opens the scroll and dramatically announces the beginning of His ministry by reading from the much loved book of Isaiah...

"The Spirit of the Lord is upon Me, because He has anointed Me to preach the gospel to the poor; He has sent Me to heal the broken-hearted, to proclaim liberty to the captives and recovery of sight to the blind, to set at liberty those who are oppressed; to proclaim the acceptable year of the Lord." Luke 4:18–19 NKJV

He then rolls up the scroll and says,

"Today this Scripture is fulfilled in your hearing." Luke 4:21 NKJV

The rest, as they say, is history.

I think it is fair to say that 'under–shepherds' who are called to represent Him should have that same heart. Much of the church is not fit for service because of brokenness and, until we acknowledge and grasp this, we will never truly get to know the Great Shepherd as the Healer and the Deliverer. Jesus commanded His disciples to preach the good news, heal the sick, cast out demons, and raise the dead.[260] This is very much the bread of the children[261] and the children desperately need that bread. Jesus told His disciples to go into all the nations and make more disciples, teaching them to obey everything He had commanded them to obey.[262] Sadly in many cases we have reduced the great commission to preaching the good news, trusting that this might accomplish the rest without our involvement. If your heart is to move forward with God and there is an issue or issues that keep you 'locked down' then please, continue to press in to the Healer and Deliverer. Never give up.

"What is impossible with man is possible with God." Jesus said that![263]

To which Simon, Julie and Ruth say: *"Amen!"*

Some probing questions:

- Is there an area, or areas of brokenness that has you 'locked down'?

  (If not then please ignore the rest of the questions!)

- Do you know the root cause of the issue, or issues?

- Could the root be rejection? abuse? grief? shame? guilt? fear? occult?

- What's the worst thing anyone ever said to you?

- What's the worst thing anyone ever did to you?

- What is your biggest, hardly dare to mention it, fear?

- If you could erase one thing out of your lifetime, what would it be?

- Do you need to forgive someone? Or yourself? Or even 'forgive' God in the sense you need to withdraw your judgment of Him?

- Will you bring the pain in the root cause to Jesus for healing?

TEN
Hearing God

Let's start with a foundational declaration. It is God's heart and God's will, that we—His beloved children—are able to receive communication from Him. When Moses led the Children of Israel out of Egypt and through the wilderness the Lord went ahead of them using a cloud by day and fire by night.[264] This is a physical picture of the spiritual, and the Apostle Paul unpacked this example to reveal it was the pre–incarnate Christ who accompanied them on their journey.

> *For I do not want you to be ignorant of the fact, brothers and sisters, that our ancestors were all under the cloud and that they all passed through the sea. They were all baptized into Moses in the cloud and in the sea. They all ate the same spiritual food and drank the same spiritual drink; for they drank from **the spiritual rock that accompanied them, and that rock was Christ**.* 1 Corinthians 10:1–4 [emphasis mine]

Jesus says to every disciple, "Follow Me,"[265] and He would not say that unless His disciples could hear His voice and follow Him. He is our Shepherd and we are His sheep.[266]

> *My sheep listen to My voice; I know them, and they follow Me.* John 10:27

> God has a plan for your life, but He will not set His detailed step–by–step plan before you for your approval.

The former chapters have hopefully begun to get your heart and your mind into a strong position in Christ, ready to do His will. This is vital. I remember as a young Christian, eager to be a disciple, eager to hear God's voice, hanging on every word as I listened to Tom Bathgate teach on this subject. To my dismay he said, *"God will not reveal His will to those who want to know it."* My head dropped. 'What was the point then?' I thought. After leaving a professional teacher's pregnant pause he delivered the key line, and my heart leapt within me. *"He reveals it to those who want to do it!"* I understood.

God has a plan for your life,[267] but He will not set His detailed step–by–step plan before you for your approval. It's not a case of His waiting for your "yes", "no" or "maybe" on each line, somewhat like choosing a meal from an a–la–carte menu. Imagine this conversation. *"Lord, I like steps 1 and 2, but sorry, I'll have to give step 3 a miss. I love step 4, can't wait for that one, but Lord, step 5, could you imagine what my spouse would say to that one!"* That's not really going to happen in any shape or form, is it? No, *should you choose to*, you count the cost,[268] and sign up in your heart as a disciple, ready to do His will. The adventure can begin.

Then gradually, line–by–line, step–by–step He will reveal His will. In Newcastle, County Down, in Northern Ireland, there is a beautiful river called the Shimna, which tumbles down the mountainside through Tollymore forest. It is a popular walking area with many trails winding through the forest, most of which cross the river at some stage. I like what the council has done. In some places there are stone and wooden bridges, but in other places they have placed circular moulded stepping–stones across the water, which adds to the sense of adventure. Each stone is close enough to the next one to be able to reach it with reasonable care, but far enough apart so that you could not skip a step on your way across.

Following Jesus is a bit like that. You can't skip the next step and come back to it. If He has impressed on you that you are to forgive 'that person' then for you, that is *your* next step on the road. Remember that He always leads you in paths of righteousness.[269] Isaiah called it the Way of Holiness.[270] That's a big clue!

> If you never heard from God in any other way, His word is enough to guide you

It is essential to emphasize that God's primary means of speaking to us all is through His written word. Hence the devil's relentless attack on its authenticity. God assures us that if we submit to Him in *all our ways* (back to Lordship[271]) He *will* direct our paths.[272] The Psalmist describes God's written word as "a lamp for my feet, and light on my path."[273] If you never heard from God in any other way, His word is enough to guide you through life in His will.

- Do you want to know what God would say to you as a husband or a wife? Read Ephesians 5 from verse 22.

- Do you want to know what God would say to you as a businessman? Read Proverbs 11:1.

- Or as an employer or employee? Read Colossians 4:1 and 3:22–23.

You get the idea! All the basic Kingdom guidance is there, ready and waiting, and easy to understand. If we don't respond to the ample God–given basic Kingdom guidelines, why would God speak to us beyond that? To the obedient and hungry heart, to the one who wants to *do* His will, to the one with ears to hear what the Spirit is saying,[274] there will be times when God illuminates a particular portion of Scripture and you know, *deep within you*, you know, that this is especially relevant *for you*. A rhema word. A verse or portion of Scripture that the Holy Spirit brings to your attention regarding a current situation or the need for direction.

Several years after I became a Christian, God illuminated a verse in Exodus so clearly and consistently that I began to understand His plan for my life, and to this day that Scripture is to be found on our ministry banner and at the base of our ministry notepaper. That Scripture two decades later still keeps me focused.

> *Then the Lord said to Moses, "Rise early in the morning and stand before Pharaoh, and say to him, 'thus says the Lord God of the Hebrews: "***Let My people go, that they may serve Me***.* " Exodus 9:13 NKJV [emphasis mine]

In Old Testament 'types', Pharaoh stands for the devil—whom Jesus referred to several times as 'the ruler of this world'[275]—and I knew that I was being called to be a co–worker with Jesus[276] in seeing His people set free from bondages and burdens that would hinder them from serving Him.[277]

As a young Christian I remember being blessed by a children's talk given in church. The minister was teaching the children how to hear from God, and it proved to be a valuable starting point for me. He had drawn a cartoon man with noise coming in through his physical ears but he had also drawn ears on the man's redeemed heart through which to hear God.

For the first time I saw it! We would never think of saying, "I asked Jesus into my mind," but would naturally say "I asked Jesus into *my heart.*" I understood that it was not my physical heart—which is a pump—but into my innermost being. The very heart of me. I could ask myself the question, *"What might God be speaking into my heart?"* That made it nice and simple for me. Here's the more complex version! We are fearfully and wonderfully made in God's image, and as He is One, and yet Three, we are also, one and yet three. *Spirit, soul and body.* It has been well said by many preachers that we are spiritual beings with a soul and we live in a body. The apostle Paul confirms this human trinity.

> *May God Himself, the God of peace, sanctify you through and through. May **your whole spirit, soul and body** be kept blameless at the coming of our Lord Jesus Christ.* 1 Thessalonians 5:23 [emphasis mine]

In what is often referred to as the Magnificat, or 'Mary's song', the opening line reveals the whole of Mary's being in worship.

*And **Mary** said: "**My soul** glorifies the Lord and **my spirit** rejoices in God my Savior."* Luke 1:46–47 [emphasis mine]

Your 'invisible' heart is the very core of your being. It has been described as the seat of your emotions, will and conscience, and your true character. Most importantly it is the connection between your spirit and soul. My understanding is that when God imparts a truth by His Spirit into your spirit, it registers in your heart while your mind is immediately aware of what your heart has just understood. So heart and spirit are closely linked as God's avenue of communication. Sometimes 'spirit' and 'heart' seem to be almost interchangeable terms.[278] Many times your *spirit* and soul is spoken of as your *'heart* and soul'.[279] Sometimes 'spirit, soul and body' are spoken of as 'heart and soul and strength'.[280] It follows that a hardened heart,[281] or a sinful and unbelieving heart,[282] or a perverse[283] or deceitful heart [284] will not be sensitive to that deep, quiet Spirit–to–spirit communication, so we must always guard our hearts[285] to make sure our hearts remain pure,[286] humble,[287] clear of anger and malice[288] and under the Lordship of Jesus.[289]

Here's a good example of your spirit, soul and body in action. Your mind can pray and sing with understanding, and the words come out through your mouth. That is your soul and body in action. If you have the gift of tongues,[290] you will know you can pray (and sing) with your spirit, *fully bypassing your mind's understanding,* and again the words will come out through your mouth. That is your spirit and body in action. The illustration below might help.

> Your 'invisible' heart
>
> is the very core
>
> of your being...
>
> Most importantly
>
> it is the connection
>
> between your
>
> spirit and soul.

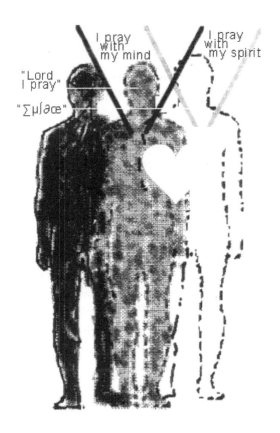

So what shall I do? I will pray with my spirit, but I will also pray with my understanding; I will sing with my spirit, but I will also sing with my understanding. 1 Corinthians 14:15

We see through a glass darkly[291], but it can be helpful to also see our *body* as a trinity (bones, flesh and blood) our *soul* as a trinity (mind – I think, emotions – I feel, and will – I do) and our *spirit* as a trinity (ability to interact with the Spirit of God, conscience and creative centre)

Every child born has a conscience and although this is God–given, it is not God. Non–Christians are just as aware of their conscience when it indicates right and wrong. They may choose to do what is right, or they may sear their consciences by overriding the clear warning.[292] Obviously a God–redeemed conscience plays a very important role in alerting us to clear issues of right and wrong. However so often we need 'delicate' guidance that has no moral right or wrong and is not specifically covered through His Word. God is Spirit,[293] and though He can speak to us in any way He chooses—emphasized by Him once using a donkey[294] and once a finger writing on a wall[295]—He normally communicates Spirit–to–spirit.[296] We could even say Heart–to–heart. As a basic communication in this area Jesus imparts His peace when we are in His will.[297] He can check our spirit or remove His peace when we are about to make the wrong decision.[298]

The most dramatic example of this I can give occurred in July 2004 in Australia. Hearing God this way saved my life! I had taught in Australia the previous July and was talking with the Regional Director about dates and subjects for a return visit the following July, when I noticed that I had lost my inner peace. My mind could not understand why, because next to Ireland, Australia is my favourite country. (As I write, I count that I have taught there eight times in nine years.) I told the Regional Director I believed God did not want me to return in July 2005 and he was as surprised as I was. I asked for time to consider but that did not change anything. I had lost my peace and had a choice to make. Go the following year because I dearly wanted to, or trust God's Spirit–to–spirit inner witness and not go. I made the right choice, and July 2005 was left free in my diary.

Then in May 2005 a friend offered us the use of her apartment in Paris for the first two weeks in July and, as that was still free in my diary, we initially accepted. Within hours I noticed I had again lost my inner peace, and so, still puzzled, we cancelled this plan to travel to Paris. On July 6th, I felt ill and, at my wife's insistence, I went to my doctor. After checking my pulse and doing an ECG, the young stand–in doctor advised me to go to the hospital for a check–up. I felt fine and seriously considered not going, but praise God my wife again insisted! As I stood talking to the receptionist in the Ulster hospital, I suddenly started shivering dramatically, and the rest, as they say is history. A virus had hit my heart and within 24 hours, my wife was told that I was being kept alive, "15 minutes at a time," and that it was unlikely I would live more than 24 hours in total. I was now in an induced coma, being kept alive by a heart machine and a large team of doctors. My kidneys and liver had stopped functioning, and my heart was pumping extremely erratically at only 10% of its volume. There was nothing they could do about it. On July 7th in a desperate attempt to save me, I was flown to Freeman's Hospital in England—in a specially hired–in Lear jet from Luxembourg—for a possible heart transplant. As you've probably guessed, God was already well ahead me and I never did get any surgery. Some of the nurses called me the 'miracle man', and a consultant said that I was 'an interesting case'. The two months in hospital in England and Ireland were life–changing in many ways. Had I not heard God I would have died in July 2005. *It is good to hear God!*

As you will have gathered, the idea here is that we hear God with our spirit, and then decide with our minds whether to obey or not. Whatever we decide, our body will then proceed to do. Again, perhaps an illustration might help.

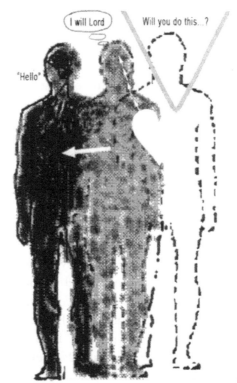

Example.

At a small Christian meeting one evening, I felt the Lord gently place into my spirit the understanding that He was asking me to put a bank check for a large amount of money into the collection bowl at the end of the evening. My mind was not rejoicing over this and my emotions were all over the place. My will had no idea what to do until I would 'make up my mind.' I paced up and down for many minutes. Would I? Yes? No? Then I made up my mind to do it. I said, 'Yes, Lord.' My emotions settled and my will moved me into action. That obedience brought me unexpected blessings. But that's another story!

Starting in Genesis,[299] Scripture is awash with two–way interaction between God and man. So there may be times when you understand God's Spirit and your spirit are having an active two–way interaction.

This happened to me in the middle of a cold and stormy December night as I was camped just below a mountaintop in the Mourne Mountains. For about fifteen minutes God's Spirit spoke into my spirit and I was aware of my innermost responses to Him. During one part of that 'conversation' I was aware He was calling me to be a teacher. Despite the fearful storm threatening to tear my tent apart, I smiled to myself. I had a stammer. A stammer so bad I found it difficult to say my own name, and almost impossible to say my wife's name. It was crippling and embarrassing, and speaking to strangers made it worse than usual. I understood Moses' initial response to God at the burning bush when he told His Maker he was not a good speaker![300] In the natural I could not see any way of becoming a Bible teacher. However, it did begin to focus my heart and mind in that direction and I soon realized I had a real love for God's word. In addition, I always found it relatively easy to understand what the Old Testament physical stories were modelling for us in the New Testament spiritual.[301] Today, two decades later, I have taught His Word in nearly twenty nations. My stammer is long gone.

We understand that God 'speaks' quietly into our spirit, because we never say, "I'm going for a noisy time with the Lord." Rather we say, "I'm going for a quiet time with the Lord." He leads us beside quiet waters.[302] During those quiet times we often sense that inner stillness, that oneness in spirit with God[303] and, as we 'move on with God', we need to learn to hold on to that inner stillness throughout the day. Remember the Lord's word to us?

He says, "Be still, and know that I am God." Psalm 46:10a

The Old Testament type as a lesson couldn't be clearer. In 1 Kings we read of Elijah sheltering in a cave and the Lord calling him to the entrance.

*Then He said, "Go out, and stand on the mountain before the Lord." And behold, the Lord passed by, and a great and strong wind tore into the mountains and broke the rocks in pieces before the Lord, but the Lord was not in the wind; and after the wind an earthquake, but the Lord was not in the earthquake; and after the earthquake a fire, but the Lord was not in the fire; and after the fire **a still small voice**.* 1 Kings 19:11–12 NKJV [emphasis mine]

The great storm would certainly grab your attention, but God was not in that. The earthquake would certainly grab your attention, but God was not in that. The fire would certainly grab your attention, but God was not in that. Then comes the revelation. The still small voice. *That was God speaking.* God will not compete with 'other voices' to get your attention. He is God and He will not play second fiddle. He is jealous for your love and your devotion.[304] I'm sure that makes sense. Knowing this, can you see why 'the god of this world'[305] will keep 'noise' in your life, will keep you 'entertained', easily bored and ill–at–ease with quality silence and prayerful contemplation? He is desperate to ensure God's people will not hear that 'still small voice' within.

I liken listening out for God's voice to emails and the internet. In the early days of noisy dial–up modems, you would dial up the internet perhaps once in the morning and then again in the evening, to see if there were any emails for you. Today, we have broadband connections open to the internet all day, every day, so emails arrive with a faint 'ding' almost as soon as they leave the sender. Some Christians are like dial–up modems. They might succeed in quieting their soul and becoming spiritually aware during their morning and evening Bible study and prayer 'quiet times', with a very real possibility of hearing from God during those specific times. When the Apostle Paul spoke of praying without ceasing[306] I like to think that his prayerful heart was an open 'broadband connection' to God all day, every day. That is how I *try* to live, so that should God choose to speak to me, anywhere at any time, I might be open and sensitive to that still small voice within.

Many times I'm sure you may have experienced God stirring your spirit within you during a particular sermon or a teaching, as if He was speaking to you and you alone.[307] Other times perhaps this has happened when you have been reading a book. (Maybe even this one!)

God can, and often will, communicate with you through the things you are in tune with. If you love music, He can speak to you through that. Or art. Or mathematics. Or pottery.[308] Or gardening. When God wanted to lead the astronomers to the Babe at Bethlehem, He sent a star.[309] If you have read my book, *Loved Like Never Before*, you will remember that God spoke to me through the great outdoors.

I once heard an audible voice say, "Just like Joseph," and once my wife heard an audible voice: "Gideon." In both cases, these words led to important revelations. As I write this, my wife and I have been Christians for a combined total of 46 years, so this is not an everyday occurrence!

Dreams and visions.[310] God can and does communicate through dreams[311] and visions.[312] But perhaps a word of warning. It can take a while before your discernment is truly matured through experience. When I was a young Christian— really 'on fire' for Jesus—my imagination was also fired up and it produced many spiritual type dreams that turned out to have nothing to do with God communicating with me! (More about that later.) When I realized this, I resolved to learn how to tune in to God *with my spirit* and, for approximately two years, God did communicate with me several times using 'cinema–like' pictures and visions while I was fully awake. Why did these stop after approximately two years? I'm not sure, but my best guess is that by then I was more able to discern His voice in my spirit. So, outside of His word, that became the main way from that point onwards. My own experience—*and that is what I am passing on*—is that when God does use a picture, dream or vision, He usually reveals the understanding of it.

For example, one morning I had a vision, not a dream, not a picture, but a full screen 3D 'you are there' vision. In the middle of an otherwise empty room there was an old pine table and, on that table, there was a lit candle set in an old fashioned candleholder. That was the only light source. Close to the candle's flame it was bright, then less and less bright, until there was gloom and finally darkness around the edges of the scene. My focus was on the candle and the flame and its light. However I had no understanding of why I was being shown this. In my heart I was asking Jesus for understanding, but there was no response. Yet the scene would not go away.

Eventually my gaze moved from the candle towards the gloom—and then I saw them! Hideous–looking demonic beings that were flashing into the gloom and then quickly back into the darkness. I immediately understood what God was saying to me. Satan and his demonic followers are chained in darkness, awaiting judgment.[313] Satan's dominion is called the dominion of darkness[314]. As we walk in the light, as Jesus is The Light,[315] they can gain no legal rights over us.[316] That's why Satan had to tempt Adam and Eve.[317] He had no authority over them until they willingly stepped into his sinful, rebellious territory. Make sure you live in the Light and walk in the Light![318]

Then there is wisdom. Not the world's wisdom[319] but God–given wisdom.[320] As a young Christian, I ministered for several years under a powerful anointing for deliverance. Accompanying this was the gift of discernment and often words of knowledge. I saw so many dramatic things happening week in and week out, I came to think this was God's complete answer to every problem. I was wrong. I came to realize what I needed most was divine wisdom. Bucket loads of it! For a year I prayed and prayed and prayed for wisdom. That's what God's word said to do.

*If any of you lacks wisdom, **you should ask God**, who gives generously to all without finding fault, and it will be given to you.* James 1:5 [emphasis mine]

When someone would offer to pray for me, I would always say, 'Pray for wisdom!' I would often get down on my knees as they prayed in order to show God just how serious I was! One day I noticed that this burden for wisdom had gone and people began saying things like, 'Can we have a piece of your wisdom?' Then I was asked to serve on a major international ministry advisory group for several years. So many times since then—particularly when faced with difficult prayer ministry and leadership decisions—I have experienced that precious wisdom. Yes, pray for wisdom. God appeared to Solomon in a dream and offered to give him anything he wanted,[321] and was greatly pleased when he asked for wisdom.[322] I think he was already wise to ask for wisdom!

> The mind is a battlefield, and whatever we give our mind to is what masters us.

God can guide our thoughts (as with His wisdom) and communicate through our mind. *However* it is important to understand that, while we have 'the mind of Christ' in position,[323] in experience it proves to be very much a work–in–progress. Many Christians have not understood this and have taken certain thoughts as God's thoughts and made mistakes. (Been there, done that!)

Type the word 'thoughts' into a Bible search website and, in the New Testament, you will see that, in most cases, they are referred to by Jesus and the Apostles in a negative sense.[324] The mind is open to myriad thoughts from

- *the world* around us[325]—the media, society, friends
- *the flesh*—our own carnal desires and our culture–shaped, self–centred nature and mindset[326]
- our past experiences and of course by thoughts from
- the devil—the prince of the power of the air.[327]

The mind is a battlefield, and whatever we give our mind to is what masters us.[328] Is it the world, the flesh, the devil or Jesus, or a mixture? In developing discernment in this area, it is important we are not conformed to the world's mindset or worldview.[329] The apostle Paul tells us to have *our* minds—*our* thinking—transformed, so that we start coming in to line with, and can more readily discern, God's good and perfect will.[330] What we might call a Biblical worldview.[331]

If your mindset has been subtly shaped by society's opinion against God's Word,[332] then that contra–mindset will be a strong blockage. Your mind will be well out of tune with the Lord. In the natural, if you place two pendulum–type grandfather clocks close to each other, the pendulums will eventually begin to swing together. *If they are close enough*. If two guitars are placed close to each other, plucking one string will resonate with a string on the other guitar. *If they are in tune*. You get the idea!

As you mature in this area, learning to take every thought captive and make it obedient to Christ,[333] you will eventually experience 'a sound mind'.[334] You will begin to sense His 'voice' in the quietness of your mind. While you're working on this with the Holy Spirit, always remember that God alone has access to our redeemed and awakened, born–again spirit.[335] That's the safe place.

Sometimes there are long silences accompanied by a zero sense of that empowering closeness—that oneness in spirit[336]—with God.

It is easy to walk closely with Jesus when His Spirit is very much in evidence within your life, but a real test comes when this is not so. Will you still walk the same path, and still hold fast to your Christian integrity?[337] If you have eaten His Word and digested it until it has become 'flesh'[338] then you can do little else as, knowing God's grace in your life, it would be an offence to your own conscience.[339] (I have heard this season in a believer's life referred to as 'the cold steel walk') At other times it can be because the silence is to emphasize the next thing you hear from Him. Your hunger grows and the ears of your heart become desperate to hear from Him.[340]

When the Old Testament closed after the book of Malachi, there was a four–century silence, because the next thing that God would say would be monumental. Matthew, chapter one. Introducing the long awaited

Messiah.[341] Sometimes it can be because there is un–confessed sin in your life.[342] Sometimes because your heart has been captivated by other things and has become lukewarm.[343] I'm sure you understand! If we love Jesus we will obey Him. If we don't we won't.[344] We go out of tune. Out of sync. We no longer have ears to hear anything but the voice of the god of this world. (You see now why the earlier chapters are so important.) Sometimes the blockage can be brokenness. I have observed that *sometimes* a person who wasn't spoken to much by their earthly father can find it difficult to believe their Heavenly Father, maker of heaven and earth, would want to communicate with them. If that's you, at the risk of repeating myself, please read my first book![345]

Let me both warn and encourage you. When I was first saved, I honestly believed that I was hearing from God fairly regularly, especially about my jointly–owned business. As I was continually trying to prove to my then long–suffering atheist business partner that God was real, I used these regular words and revelations—which came from dreams or warm thoughts about the business while I was reading the Bible—to prophecy to him about what was going to happen in the business.

How did that work out? After two years my accuracy rate proved to be nil. Zero. Nothing. It was then I realized God wasn't making mistakes. It was me! I was thinking these were all from Him when they clearly were not. I was disheartened. The words 'loose cannon' began to enter my thinking. Slowly but surely I calmed down, got over my disappointment—and yes, my embarrassment—and started afresh. Patiently, very patiently, I began to get more in tune with Jesus. My success rate in hearing God, and thus my credibility with those who knew me, slowly increased.

I was no longer a potential loose cannon in the Body of Christ. It was a hard lesson, but an essential one. Over the years I have had quite a few well–meaning Christians bring me a variety of 'words from the Lord', which I knew immediately—through the check in my spirit—were not from the Lord.

> Maturity is a process, not a microwave operation!

I have seen some very destructive mistakes. Many people brought the same word to a lovely Christian lady in her early fifties and single: "The Lord is preparing a man for you and you will meet him shortly." What was happening was they loved this Godly lady and felt sorry for her. When they thought of her being married it produced a warm emotional response and they mistook this as the Lord confirming their thoughts. More than a decade later it has never happened.

Then there was a man who stopped a married couple as they emerged from their wedding service to give them 'a word from the Lord' that the next two years were going to be very difficult. How's that for a wedding present, just minutes after you get married? It ruined their honeymoon and it was only when the first two years were up they realized they could be free of this word.

> If God has been speaking to you, a true word will confirm what He has already been witnessing to you.

Another example: the expectant mother of four sons who is told that 'the Lord says' this will be their long–awaited daughter, and it turns out to be a fifth son. A girl's name had been picked, a room decorated pink. There was confusion and shock, cries of "It can't be! It's meant to be a girl."

All these mistakes created prime openings for the serpent.[346] So be humble, be teachable, be submissive to mature Christians, be hungry for the Lord and be ready to be pruned when necessary.[347] It is worth it. Maturity is a process, not a microwave operation!

On the other hand, the Lord has indeed used Christians to bring a genuine word to me. In these cases I have always had a clear witness within my spirit.

After 23 years as a committed Christian, I estimate the accuracy rate of words given to me by other believers as being around the 20% mark. Your experience may be different. John Bevere's book *Thus Saith the Lord* is worth reading in this regard.[348]

Never make a major decision based only on someone's 'word from the Lord'. If God has been speaking to you, a true word will confirm what He has already been witnessing to you. Getting it wrong can bring heartache in its wake. If you feel increasingly confident God is directing you towards a major decision, pray for definite and unmistakable confirmation. Remember Gideon.[349] When I believed God was calling me to leave employment to serve Him full time in December 1994, I asked Him for—and got—not one, not two, but three clear confirmations. I left employment and never doubted from that moment that God had spoken to me.

The next section is devoted to helping you discern the difference between the Lord's voice and the voice of the enemy. In the early days I was duped in this area and it was distressing. I am embarrassed to write these, but the following stories might help to illustrate the point.

I had read that a lady in America had been asked by the Lord to give her lovely home to a homeless couple and she did. Guess what? A month or two later I believed the Lord was coldly, determinately and persistently asking me to do the same. It was 'a command' that seemed to hang like a heavy cloak around me day and night. I wanted to obey Him but I could not find any inner strength to do this, so I sank into great condemnation. So much so I stepped aside from wanting to serve Him since I was now—in my own eyes—a total failure as a Christian, and as a disciple. I was in torment for two weeks until one afternoon as I was walking back down a mountainside, the 'real' Lord spoke lovingly into my spirit and assured me that had not been his voice, but the deceiving voice of the enemy.[350] A painful lesson indeed.

But again it happened. I was waiting to turn right in busy city traffic, when suddenly a terrible blasphemous thought about the Holy Spirit hit my mind. It was quickly followed by the accusation—as I thought from God—that I had blasphemed the Holy Spirit[351] and was now beyond redemption. No words can describe the next three months of my life.

> If you are worried that you have blasphemed the Holy Spirit, then that is the proof that you have not.

This hung over me like death itself. The more I cried out to God for forgiveness, the worse it seemed to get! I didn't tell anyone what I was going through, as I thought no one could help me. I thought myself destined to live my life with only hell waiting at the end of it. Then one day, in a bookshop, I picked up a small booklet on the Holy Spirit and noticed that there was a section on blaspheming the Holy Spirit. I hardly dared open it, but I did. It said that, if you are worried that you have blasphemed the Holy Spirit, then that is the proof that you have not, because if the Holy Spirit had truly departed from your life, you would not have the slightest interest in salvation, and would be deeply attracted to darkness. I understood that, and suddenly the tormenting spirit left me, and I was free. Again, what a powerful lesson on my journey!

Sometimes I ask an audience to raise their hands if at some stage in their early walk with God, Satan deceived them into believing they had committed the 'unpardonable sin'. The average response is usually about one third of the people raising their hands; each shocked to see they were not the only one! So reader, if *you* think *you* have, *you* haven't!

So here goes.

A comparison to help you know the difference between the two 'voices.'

This is substantially based on a paper I found many years ago which said 'author unknown', so Author Unknown, whoever you are, thank you.

The Holy Spirit	The accuser of the brethren
1. The tone of voice is kind and gentle and peaceable. It is the loving, patient voice of Our Father. It is that still small voice.	The voice of Satan is 'loud'. An accusing, nagging, mocking voice, generating fear, causing confusion, projecting a sense of rejection.

The Holy Spirit	The accuser of the brethren
2. The Holy Spirit is ALWAYS specific about what has grieved Him. That is: When you put this ONE THING right you will be free of the conviction. The conviction carries no sense of condemnation.	Satan's voice is vague and general. 'You've done wrong and God is angry with you. You're in trouble; you've offended God.' He does not point out that one issue and show you the one way out. There is a blanketing, choking sense of general guilt. A sense of hopelessness and weakness develops with no end in sight. You start throwing repentance prayer darts at the board hoping to hit the issue but you never score a bull's eye. "Lord whatever I've done, I'm sorry."
3. The Holy Spirit is your encourager.	Satan's voice is always discouragement. He centres his attack on you as a person. "You're no good." "You always get it wrong." "You're a disappointment to God." Shame, guilt, condemnation, despair etc.
4. The Holy Spirit assures you that the past is dealt with; you are forgiven. Christ's righteousness is yours.	Remember your past. Remember the people you let down, the people you hurt, the damage you caused. "Do you *really* believe that Holy God has forgiven *you*?" Satan speaks of God as your cruel merciless judge.

The Holy Spirit	The accuser of the brethren
5. With the Holy Spirit there is always an attraction *towards* God. He generates an expectancy of love, forgiveness and a fresh start.	Satan *disguises himself as an agent of holiness* projecting the impression that God has rejected you as unworthy and unholy; and you shrink back from God.
6. The Holy Spirit brings positive Scriptures to your remembrance. He speaks of the unchanging nature of God; of His steadfast love towards us, and His faithfulness to His covenant.	Satan brings negative Scriptures to your mind. Shakespeare said "the devil knows how to quote Scripture to his purpose." Satan says grace is denied because you didn't fulfil the conditions. Satan uses the law against you to justify yourself and to strive to rely on your own righteousness before God.
7. The Holy Spirit draws you into fellowship and brings others along to minister to you in genuine love, thus you learn to accept others words of encouragement and to appreciate others.	Satan isolates you. He causes you to withdraw from other Christians with a mindset that they reject you. In your isolation you then feel lonely, unworthy and angry. Despair soon sets in, followed by hopelessness. Even suicidal thoughts.
8. The conviction of the Holy Spirit brings you truth about your relationship with God and feelings must follow facts.	Satan works by feelings. He tells you that the way you feel is the way things are. That is: "feelings are truth". Feelings of guilt, hopelessness, despair, feelings of doubt about God's love for you, feelings of God's unfairness and partiality.
9. The Holy Spirit brings discipline to draw you close to Himself as a Father disciplines his child.	Satan's 'discipline' drives you down and away from God as a cruel father would do.

The Holy Spirit	The accuser of the brethren
10. The Holy Spirit brings you comfort and assurance that—even when you are shocked at our own faithlessness—nothing can separate you from the love of God.	Satan will fire a blasphemous thought into your mind and immediately accuse you of committing the unpardonable sin.

Let's finish this long chapter with an appropriate scripture.

But when He, the Spirit of truth, comes, He will guide you into all truth. John 16:13

Some probing questions:

• Have you been aware of God speaking to you?

• What means did He use?

• How did you respond?

• Are you aware of your spirit?[352]

• What have you learnt from this chapter?

ELEVEN
Growing Pains!

In the natural we start life as babies, infants and children, then gradually grow into strong young sons and daughters, and finally—if all goes to plan—into mature adults. Our four children are now fully grown and matured adults, but they were not always that way. Our Christian life is a similar journey.

When I became a Christian at the adult age of forty–two, I was in effect a newborn child of God.[353] What the apostle Paul might call an infant[354] and the apostle Peter might call a baby.[355] I could only be fed spiritual 'milk'.[356] Baby food. Christianity–lite.

Baby Christians are lovable of course, but as most pastors will affirm, they fall down quite often and soil their nappies a lot! (Again, been there, done that!) Christian children, although enthusiastic and active, become bored easily. Church leaders often find it necessary to make services entertaining in order to keep them coming week after week.

Mature Christian sons and daughters are different. *Very different.* The world has little hold on them. They are led by God's Spirit and their minds are obedient and submissive to God's Spirit. They are focused on Jesus. They want Jesus, and they want only what Jesus wants.

For as many as are led by the Spirit of God, these are sons of God.
Romans 8:14 NKJV

> To be a man of God
>
> you need to be
>
> God's man. Not the
>
> world's man.
>
> Never perfect of course,
>
> and always growing,
>
> but God's man.

They can now be called upon, and relied upon, to play a serious part in their Father's business.[357] When my first son was born, I remember running into work shouting, "I've got a son!" and of course I did have a son. But he was a baby. Now that he is in his forties, he is a son, but no longer a baby. If I were in business and he joined me, the enterprise would probably be called *Symington and Son*. You get the picture!

After years of being an obedient son or daughter, filled with the Spirit, led by the Spirit, soaked in Kingdom ways, with much and varied Kingdom experience under their belt, these 'sons' may be surprised to find that they are now regarded as men and women of God. Moses *grew* into a man of God.[358] As did Samuel,[359] and as did David,[360] to name but three. With many growing pains along the way! This is your goal. To grow up into Christ and become a strong oak where many sheep and lambs can safely shelter.[361] A living example to those coming behind you.[362] A spiritual 'father' to young Christians.[363] Paul addressed Timothy, his spiritual son, as a man of God.

> *But you, **man of God**, flee from all this, and pursue righteousness, godliness, faith, love, endurance and gentleness. Fight the good fight of the faith. Take hold of the eternal life to which you were called when you made your good confession in the presence of many witnesses.*
> 1 Timothy 6:11–12 [emphasis mine]

To be a man of God you need to be *God's man*. Not the world's man. Or even—dare I say it—your denomination's man. God's man. Never perfect of course, and always growing, but God's man. You can't be bought or sold. The praise of men, or the animosity of men will not quell your love for Jesus, for His people, or for His call on your life. Will you know if and when you get there? Yes. When the testing comes all will be revealed. Ask Peter.[364]

Back to young Christians. They are easy to identify because they are usually still a 'mixture'. Loving Jesus, yet still at ease watching things on TV that sent Jesus to the cross. Loving Jesus, yet still full of strong opinions that contradict God's clear revelation through Scripture. Loving Jesus, yet perhaps still struggling with the idea of submission to church leaders.[365] Loving Jesus, yet still struggling with discernment over what is good and what is evil. (Think of how many Christians joined the world in embracing Harry Potter and his 'good' witchcraft![366]) Loving Jesus, but not always living as 'clean' children.[367] Listen to the apostle Paul speaking to Christians as children, and telling them how to grow into the spiritual authority of mature sons and daughters.

> *As a fair exchange—**I speak as to my children**—open wide your hearts also. Do not be yoked together with unbelievers. For what do righteousness and wickedness have in common? Or what fellowship can light have with darkness? What harmony is there between Christ and Belial? Or what does a believer have in common with an unbeliever? What agreement is there between the temple of God and idols? For we are the temple of the living God. As God has said: "I will live with them and walk among them, and I will be their God, and they will be my people." Therefore, **"Come out from them and be separate, says the Lord. Touch no unclean thing, and I will receive you." And, "I will be a Father to you, and you will be my sons and daughters, says the Lord Almighty."*** 2 Corinthians 6:13–18 [emphasis mine]

The idea is that we deal with 'mixture'[368] in our lives. The idea is that we walk with Jesus as our guide, *and Him alone.*

It might be helpful if we start at the very beginning. Right back with Adam when he walked and talked with God 'in the cool of the day.'[369] At the risk of repeating truths in the previous chapter, this simple illustration might help. It shows a clean, clear line of communication. The Holy Spirit could speak to Adam's spirit, and then his soul— originally in perfect submission to God—would have instantly obeyed whatever was on God's heart. Simple and straight–forward. God would lead and Adam would follow. Jesus, the last Adam,[370] continually modelled this relationship for us.[371]

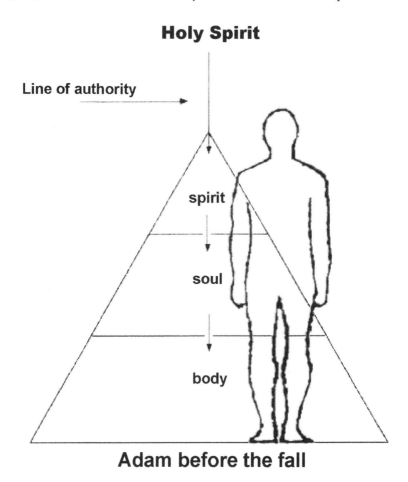

Holy Spirit

Line of authority

spirit

soul

body

Adam before the fall

Adam and Eve had the freedom and privilege to enjoy God's fellowship and His creation, with just one important condition. God alone would decide what was good and what was evil. That was the one tree they were not to eat the fruit of.[372] We know what happened, and what is still happening. Satan persuaded Adam and Eve to intentionally disobey God. To step out from under God's rule, and to be the ruler over their own lives.[373] What Satan didn't tell them of course, was that in going their own way they were going his way! They had simply swopped spiritual rulers.[374] Sin (disobedience) closed down their precious spirit–to–Spirit link with God[375] and, thinking they were doing it 'their way', they now came under the very subtle, but very real, rule of the powers of darkness.[376] Satan— working through Adam's God–given authority—became the evil ruler of this world.[377] He still works through Adam's seed the same way.[378] Read the papers. Watch the news. Look around at society. It is real.

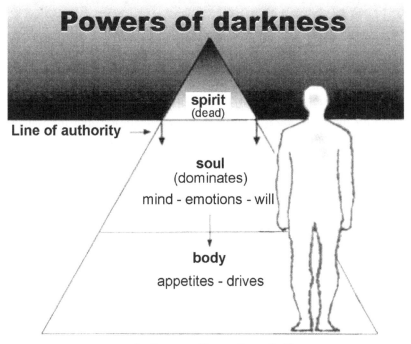

Adam after the fall

Instead of God's plans and purposes being outworked through mankind it became Satan's plans and purposes being outworked through mankind. Now the good news! When we were wonderfully saved—*our trespasses fully forgiven through the shed Blood of Jesus*—our born again spirit could resume its original created purpose.[379] Alive again to God's Spirit.[380] God's rule on earth could once again be outworked through us, His obedient children. That is His heart for us,[381] but experience shows that this does not happen immediately, and—after an excited honeymoon period—many of us realize that we, His beloved children, are not yet His obedient children. Many of us have simply moved from being worldly–minded and unsaved, to worldly–minded and saved. *Still infants!*

> *Brothers and sisters, I could not address you as people who live by the Spirit but as people who are **still worldly—mere infants in Christ.** I gave you milk, not solid food, for you were not yet ready for it. Indeed, you are still not ready. **You are still worldly.** For since there is jealousy and quarrelling among you, are you not worldly? Are you not acting like mere humans?* 1 Corinthians 3:1–3

In growing up and moving on with God there is much to do. Battles to be fought and won. Inner battles first. The old self to be put off, reckoned as crucified with Christ,[382] and the new self put on. In this next portion of Scripture the words <u>underlined</u> are what God has already done for us in our secure salvation position, while the words ***in bold italics*** are what *we* are called to work with the Holy Spirit on *after we are saved.*

> <u>*Since, then, you have been raised with Christ,*</u> ***set your hearts on things above,*** <u>*where Christ is, seated at the right hand of God.*</u> ***Set your minds on things above, not on earthly things.*** <u>*For you died, and your life is now hidden with Christ in God. When Christ, who is your life, appears, then you also will appear with him in glory.*</u> ***Put to death, therefore, whatever belongs to your earthly nature: sexual immorality, impurity, lust, evil desires and greed, which is idolatry.*** *Because of these, the wrath of God is coming. You used to walk in these ways, in the life you once lived.* ***But now you must also rid yourselves of all such things as these: anger, rage, malice, slander, and filthy language from your lips. Do not lie to each other, since you have taken off your old self with its practices and have put on the new self,*** *which is being renewed in knowledge in the image of its Creator.* Colossians 3:1–10 [emphasis mine]

The New Testament speaks much about 'the flesh' warring against the spirit,[383] but of course your body's flesh, bones and blood will only do what your soul permits it to do. A dead body will confirm this! The flesh spoken of is our carnal nature. Our sensual nature. Our *what about me?'* nature. It might help to understand that our redeemed spirit is more God–conscious and our soul more self–conscious, thus on a day–to–day basis, carnal Christians are more likely to be controlled by their souls than by their spirits. So when a negative event impacts them, their first reaction is a soulish reaction. If someone slaps them on the cheek (verbally, emotionally or physically) they immediately slap back. Perhaps when evening comes, they play spiritual catch–up. As they close their eyes in prayer and begin to focus on their relationship with God, (the dial–up modem Christian) their spirit rises to the surface and they are aware of their sinful behavior during the day, and repent.

> We are called to carefully and deliberately set our mind to obey what the Spirit desires until it becomes a habit.

But the next day all is repeated. The Spirit–filled, Spirit–led Christian has a different walk. *Far from perfect of course*, but on the right track. When a negative event hits their life, there is a much better chance of a Christ–honouring spiritual reaction. We are called to carefully and deliberately set our mind to obey what the Spirit desires until it becomes a habit. A way of life.

> *Those who live according to the flesh have their minds set on what the flesh desires; but those who live in accordance with the Spirit have their minds set on what the Spirit desires.* Romans 8:5

To truly move on with God, and to walk with God day in and day out, requires that ongoing personal development whereby you walk *by the spirit*, live *in the Spirit*, and do not gratify the relentless desires of your flesh. Our heart's cry should always be, "not my will but yours be done."[384] The apostle Paul put it this way,

> So I say, **walk by the Spirit**, and you will not gratify the desires of the flesh. For the flesh desires what is contrary to the Spirit, and the Spirit what is contrary to the flesh. They are in conflict with each other, so that you are not to do whatever you want. But **if you are led by the Spirit**, you are not under the law.
>
> The acts of the flesh are obvious: sexual immorality, impurity and debauchery; idolatry and witchcraft; hatred, discord, jealousy, fits of rage, selfish ambition, dissensions, factions and envy; drunkenness, orgies, and the like. I warn you, as I did before, that those who live like this will not inherit the kingdom of God. But the fruit of the Spirit is love, joy, peace, forbearance, kindness, goodness, faithfulness, gentleness and self–control. Against such things there is no law. Those who belong to Christ Jesus have crucified the flesh with its passions and desires. **Since we live by the Spirit, let us keep in step with the Spirit**. Galatians 5:16–25 [emphasis mine]

That's worth reading again. There is the war explained, and there is the answer explained. It is worth noting the apostle Paul states that those who habitually 'do' such things will not inherit the Kingdom of God. That's a big statement! The Greek language has two words for 'do' and Paul uses 'prasso' which means to continually do as a lifestyle. Had he used the word 'poieo' it would mean an occasional act.[385]

Here's the understanding. When we were born again God's seed,[386] (Greek 'sperma') His very nature and His word, His 'DNA', was implanted into our spirit. That's why the apostle John said that whoever abides (lives) in Jesus cannot continue to wilfully practice sin.[387] Such deliberate behavior runs contrary to God's nature that has been deeply 'seeded' into us. Our old nature is fighting an ever–losing battle. The Kingdom of God has come, is coming and will come.[388] If your redeemed spirit is not grieved when you sin, or if there is not a war between your spirit and flesh, then you need to ask yourself if you are truly born again! "Since we live by the Spirit, let us keep *in step* with the Spirit." That's the key to walking with

God. How does a person ensure that their spirit to Spirit connection with God is the controlling factor in their life? I believe it was Billy Graham who told the following story. When gold was discovered in the Yukon, thousands of men rushed to the area to seek their fortune. However, rather than saving their hard–earned riches they tended to come into town on a Saturday night to drink and gamble. One man was clever enough to make a fortune without ever lifting a shovel. While the men were in the saloon drinking, he set up a fenced–off ring in the muddy street outside. When the men emerged from the saloon he would invite them to bet on his two dogs that were about to fight in the ring. A white dog, and a black dog. Even though the men were drunk they were not easy prey. They cautiously placed a little gold on one dog or the other. The white dog won easily, so next week they placed a little more gold on the white dog, and again it won easily. Now they were certain they were on to a good thing, so the following week they placed a lot of gold on the white dog. But this time the black dog won. Cautiously, the following week, they placed a little gold on the black dog, and to their delight it won easily. So the following week they placed a little more gold on the black dog and it won easily. Now—once again certain that they were on to a good thing—they placed all their gold the following week on the black dog. Yes, you've guessed it! The white dog won. On it went, backwards and forwards, week after week, until the man had enough money to retire both himself and his two dogs. He finally joined them for a drink in the saloon where the men gathered round him eager to ask him for his secret. How was he able to ensure which dog won? "That's easy," he said with a smile. *"Whichever one I fed."*

If you feed your carnal nature more, then your soul will dominate. If you feed your spirit more, then your Holy Spirit–led spirit will dominate, and you will live in God's order of spirit, soul and body.[389] That's why fasting can be so powerful. It starves your 'me' desires and allows your

How do you know when your redeemed spirit is the stronger?

By the fruit!

Disciples are known by the fruit.

spirit to rise up strongly. I try to ensure my spirit is always better fed than my soul, not only by quiet times morning and evening, but also by inwardly remaining aware of, and often meditating on, God and His word throughout the day. (The broadband connection!)

During the day I strive[390] to take each unwanted thought captive by inwardly asking myself, "Is that thought acceptable to Jesus?"[391] This becomes an easy habit eventually! At night–time, before I fall asleep, and again if I waken during the night, I often listen to Christian podcasts from teachers I find inspiring and challenging. I want the white dog to win every week, not just occasionally.

How do you know when your redeemed spirit is the stronger? By the fruit! The Spirit's personality will come forth in you as fruit.[392] Jesus is the Vine and we the branches. Disciples are known by the fruit.[393] The Scriptures speak of our salvation in three tenses. We are saved,[394] we are being saved[395] and when we die in Christ, we will be saved.[396] The 'being saved' is the *now* part, the part between salvation and 'going home'. The apostle Paul counsels us to take this part seriously.[397]

> *Therefore, my dear friends, as you have always obeyed—not only in my presence, but now much more in my absence—***continue to work out your salvation with fear and trembling***, for it is God who works in you to will and to act in order to fulfil his good purpose.* Philippians 2:12–13 [emphasis mine]

When we were unsaved and Satan was 'our father',[398] darkness had flooded into our spirit, which then brought sin into our soul, which may have adversely affected our body. As Christians, now with God as our Father,[399] Light floods into our spirit through faith,[400] and then, as we obey that Light, righteousness develops in our soul,[401] and as our soul prospers, our body can also.[402]

Obedience—*child–like obedience*—is the key to this growing process.[403] As a young child might say to their friends, "My daddy said it and that settles it!" If we love Jesus we will (as the natural outworking) obey Him. And if we don't love Him, we won't.[404] Each of us, saved and unsaved, always have

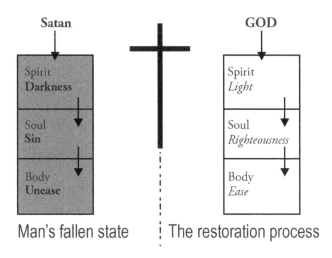

communication coming in from the world, the flesh, the devil and our past. These all combine to have a strong directional effect on the unsaved, but as Christians, these should no longer have a strong directional effect on our lives. As Christians we also have *communication from God*, and it is that precious communication—given priority—that is to be our guidance. The communication from the world, the flesh, the devil and our past needs to be immediately recognized as such, and given no authority to influence us. Quite a challenge![405] When the twelve spies returned from the Promised Land they announced to all that they were fearful of the giants who were standing on the land of their destiny.[406] All accept Joshua and Caleb. Caleb said,

> *"We should go up and take possession of the land, for we can certainly do it."* Numbers 13:30

That attitude greatly pleased God.[407] They knew that, while they could not win the battles in their own strength, with God they could—and would. However, more about that in a future chapter!

Finally, isn't it amazing that like any good father, God wants to see His children move on from crawling, to walking, to finally coming into the advancing Kingdom work as seriously useful co-workers alongside Jesus?

As God's co–workers... 2 Corinthians 6:1

How's that for an invitation to a meaningful and adventurous life?

Some probing questions:

- Would you say that you are a child or a matured son or daughter?

- Are you aware of growing pains in your Christian life?

- Which do you feed more? Your spirit or your soul?

- Did God witness anything to you during this chapter?

TWELVE
The Dark Night of the Soul

The term 'dark night of the soul' originated in a work by the sixteenth–century friar, John of the Cross. The dark night, said John, is a tortuous but fruitful path to union with God.

Many mature men and women of God will testify He had to break them before He could make them. In one form or the other this reality features in biographies on Charles Spurgeon, Martin Luther, Francis Schaeffer, Madame Guyon, Augustine, John Wesley, Watchman Nee, Catherine Marshall, Dietrich Bonhoeffer, Brother Lawrence, Hudson Taylor, Charles Finney, George Fox, William Law and Jesse Penn Lewis. Oswald Cambers wrote a poem entitled *Dark Night of the Soul.*[408]

Loren Sandford in his book *Burnout* wrote on the dark night of the soul:

> "Scripture shows us a reported pattern in which man receives a call, experiences success, is driven into exile (dark night) and then, finally returns to fulfil his destiny in the Lord." [409]

Maybe you remember these lines from the Rev. Daniel Iverson's hymn that many of us joyfully sang at meetings way back in the eighties and early nineties, not realising the seriousness of what we were singing!

> Spirit of the living God, fall afresh on me.

Spirit of the living God, fall afresh on me.

Break me, melt me, mould me, fill me.

Spirit of the living God, fall afresh on me.

Joseph was a man that God was going to use greatly, but as a young man he could possibly be accused of youthful arrogance and a great lack of wisdom and sensitivity.

Scripture describes his early years well.

> *Joseph, a young man of seventeen, was tending the flocks with his brothers, the sons of Bilhah and the sons of Zilpah, his father's wives, and he brought their father a bad report about them. Now Israel loved Joseph more than any of his other sons, because he had been born to him in his old age; and he made an ornate robe for him. When his brothers saw that their father loved him more than any of them, they hated him and could not speak a kind word to him. Joseph had a dream, and when he told it to his brothers, they hated him all the more. He said to them, "Listen to this dream I had: We were binding sheaves of grain out in the field when suddenly my sheaf rose and stood upright, while your sheaves gathered around mine and bowed down to it." His brothers said to him, "Do you intend to reign over us? Will you actually rule us?" And they hated him all the more because of his dream and what he had said. Then he had another dream, and he told it to his brothers. "Listen," he said, "I had another dream, and this time the sun and moon and eleven stars were bowing down to me." When he told his father as well as his brothers, his father rebuked him and said, "What is this dream you had? Will your mother and I and your brothers actually come and bow down to the ground before you?" His brothers were jealous of him, but his father kept the matter in mind.* Genesis 37:2–11

Joseph was thirty years old when he became Pharaoh's prime minister,[410] and from then on he ruled wisely and fulfilled his unique God–given destiny. What events helped to shape him in those intervening thirteen years? It makes for sobering reading!

First his brothers threw him into a cistern as a temporary prison, and then sold him for twenty pieces of silver to some passing Ishmaelites. They soaked his ornate coat in the blood of a goat before presenting it to their father as proof his favourite son must surely have been torn to pieces by a ferocious animal.[411] The Ishmaelites then sold Joseph to Potiphar, a captain in Pharaoh's guard, and he began a new life far from home as an Egyptian family slave. The Lord prospered Joseph in all he did and this impressed Potiphar so much he made him his personal attendant giving him rule over his entire household. Surely now God was ready to use him? *Not yet!*

Joseph was a well–built handsome young man and Potiphar's wife regularly tried to have a sexual relationship with him, but to no avail. He was immovable.

"How then could I do such a wicked thing and sin against God?" And though she spoke to Joseph day after day, he refused to go to bed with her or even be with her. Genesis 39:9–10

Joseph's integrity was being tested day after day and he was passing each test. Surely now God was ready to use him? *Not yet!*

One day Potiphar's unfaithful wife grabbed Joseph and demanded he go to bed with her. Joseph struggled free and fled from the house, leaving her clutching his cloak. This robust rejection of her advances turned her heart against Joseph and she claimed he had tried to rape her, but that she had fought him off. As evidence, she was still holding his cloak. Joseph was promptly thrown into jail accused of attempted rape! Even in jail God prospered him in everything he did, and the jailer eventually put him in charge of all prison affairs.

While in prison two former servants of Pharaoh—a baker and a cupbearer—had strange dreams for which God gave Joseph two very different interpretations. In due time the baker had his head chopped off and put on a pole, while the cupbearer was restored to his former position in Pharaoh's entourage. Exactly as Joseph had interpreted their dreams. Surely Joseph was ready? *Not yet!*

> I willingly bear witness that I owe more to my Lord's fire, hammer and file than to anything else in His workshop.

The cupbearer was grateful, but as soon as he was out of prison he forgot to mention Joseph to Pharaoh. Thirteen long lonely years far from home. First as a slave. Then as a falsely–accused rapist. A forgotten prisoner in a hot dusty eastern jail. But two years after the cupbearer left prison, all that was about to change. Pharaoh had two strange and symbolic dreams and knew they must mean something. But what? Finally (in God's timing) the cupbearer remembered Joseph and his God–given gift of interpreting dreams. Pharaoh sent for him and he was able to interpret the strange dreams to Pharaoh's complete satisfaction. So much so, that within hours Joseph suddenly found himself promoted to the second most powerful man in Egypt.[412] *Now he was ready!*

The rest is history that Scripture unpacks beautifully in Genesis chapters 42–47. The 'dark years' had slowly but surely shaped a Godly young man into a man of God and a vessel fit for use.

Charles Surgeon wrote, "I willingly bear witness that I owe more to my Lord's fire, hammer and file than to anything else in His workshop. Sometimes I wonder if I have ever learned anything except at the end of God's rod. When my classroom is darkest, I see best."

I remember as a keen young athlete reaching a running level I simply could not improve on, and it frustrated me greatly. Then someone advised me to join a running club. I did. *Ballydrain Harriers.* The tiny clubhouse was situated in the countryside, but to me, a city–bred lad, it was in the middle of nowhere! I joined in October just as the darker nights were arriving. On my first night out with the club runners, we set out from the clubhouse at a gentle pace and my fears of not being good enough subsided. We ran along tiny country roads, up laneways and back on to other tiny country roads. Then they gradually stepped up the pace and I quickly fell many meters behind. A deep primal fear set in as darkness descended and I could only stay in touch by sound and not by sight. If I lost them, I had not the slightest idea how to get back to the clubhouse! I developed ears like a bat. I could just about hear their footsteps on a distant patch of gravel, or the sound of their occasional conversations being carried in the night air. I swore that if I got back safely I would never come back.

I just managed to hang on and get back, speechless with the burning of the cold night air in my chest as it heaved violently for many minutes after I sat down with my head thrown back trying to maximize air intake. But come back next week I did. And the exact same episode unfolded. And the next week. And the next. Every week I swore I would never put myself through it again, and every week I came back. Then spring arrived and along with it came the road–racing season. To my surprise my running had improved out of all recognition, and I eventually achieved my target of a three hour marathon. (Well, three hours and thirteen seconds to be exact. That seemingly tiny 0.2 of a mile added on to the end of the 26 miles stopped me breaking through the much–coveted three–hour barrier.) There are ways darkness strengthens you that nothing else can. This applies in the spiritual. Isaiah wrote,

> *I will give you the treasures of darkness and hidden riches of secret places, that you may know that I, the Lord, who call **you** by your name, am the God of Israel.* Isaiah 45:3 NKJV

Moses was destined to be used by God. We know his story well. It has fascinated both Christian and non–Christian alike. Cecil B. De Mille made the first major film about him in 1956 and then in 1998 DreamWorks Pictures brought out an animated version called *The Prince of Egypt*. More such films will surely follow. The Moses timeline starts out well as he is raised in Pharaoh's household through adoption by one of Pharaoh's daughters.[413] Moses was called to set the Hebrew people free from bondage so that they might serve God[414]. Egypt was at the height of its power and influence. In modern terms it could be likened to 20th century USA. Thus, Moses could be likened to being raised as an adopted son of the President in the White House. He would have been raised with the best teachers, the finest fighting instructors, the wisest counsellors and the greatest orators.[415]

Surely a perfect preparation for his calling? However when Moses' sense of destiny first arose in his breast, it all went horribly wrong for him.

> *One day, after Moses had grown up, he went out to where his own people were and watched them at their hard labor. He saw an Egyptian beating a Hebrew, one of his own people. Glancing this way and that and seeing no one, he killed the Egyptian and hid him in the sand. The next day he went out and saw two Hebrews fighting. He asked the one in the wrong, "Why are you hitting your fellow Hebrew?" The man said, "Who made you ruler and judge over us? Are you thinking of killing me as you killed the Egyptian?" Then Moses was afraid and thought, "What I did must have become known." When Pharaoh heard of this, he tried to kill Moses, but Moses fled from Pharaoh and went to live in Midian…* Exodus 2:11–15

What was God doing? Was His plan not unfolding properly? Was Moses finished?

For the next forty years Moses lived in the wilderness, working as a shepherd in an area around a mountain called Horeb. Little did he know he would be called by God to shepherd His people (His 'sheep') through the wilderness, and especially to the mountain called Horeb, referred to as the *Mountain of God*. (This is an interchangeable name with Mount Sinai.[416])

The turning point in his life came when one day—one ordinary, usually predictable, somewhat boring day—he saw a bush on fire, but not being burnt! It is one of the world's best–known God encounters.

> *Now Moses was tending the flock of Jethro his father–in–law, the priest of Midian. And he led the flock to the back of the desert, and came to Horeb, the mountain of God. And the Angel of the Lord appeared to him in a flame of fire from the midst of a bush. So he looked, and behold, the bush was burning with fire, but the bush was not consumed. Then Moses said, "I will now turn aside and see this great sight, why the bush does not burn." So when the Lord saw that he turned aside to look, God called to him from the midst of the bush*

and said, "Moses, Moses!" And he said, "Here I am." Exodus 3:1–4
NKJV

The Angel of the Lord (means God Himself when the word 'angel' has a capital A) gives Moses his calling.

"...I will send you to Pharaoh that you may bring My people, the children of Israel, out of Egypt." Exodus 3:10 NKJV

Now we see what the 'dark night of the soul' was about. Listen to Moses' responses.

But Moses said to God, "Who am I that I should go to Pharaoh and bring the Israelites out of Egypt?" Exodus 3:11

Moses said to the Lord, "Pardon your servant, Lord. I have never been eloquent, neither in the past nor since you have spoken to your servant. I am slow of speech and tongue." Exodus 4:10

But Moses said, "Pardon your servant, Lord. Please send someone else." Exodus 4:13

The wilderness time had turned a man who could be rightfully confident in his many abilities into the most humble man on earth.

Now Moses was a very humble man, more humble than anyone else on the face of the earth. Numbers 12:3

Can you see what the process did to Joseph and Moses? They substantially died so that God could substantially live in them. Both cannot exist in equal measure.

John the Baptist said it well when he declared, *"He must increase, but I must decrease."* John 3:30 NKJV

Then there is Job. I often think that one of the many virtues to be found in the story of his dark night of the soul, is that no matter how dark the night might get in our lives, we can always say, "It's not as bad as Job's!"

Watchman Nee described the 'dark night' this way,

But the difficulty with many of us is that dark night. The Lord graciously laid me aside once in my life for a number of months and put me, spiritually, into utter darkness. It was almost as though He had forsaken me, almost as though nothing was going on and I had really come to the end of everything. And then by degrees He brought things back again. The temptation is always to try to help God by taking things back ourselves; but remember, there must be a full night in the sanctuary, a full night in darkness. It cannot be hurried; He knows what He is doing.

We would like to have death and resurrection put together within one hour of each other. We cannot face the thought that God will keep us aside for so long a time; we cannot bear to wait. And I cannot tell you how long He will take, but in principle I think it is quite safe to say this, that there will be a definite period when He will keep you there. It will seem as though nothing is happening; everything you valued is slipping from your grasp. There confronts you a blank wall with no door in it. Seemingly everyone else is being blessed and used, while you yourself have been passed by and are losing out. Lie quiet. All is in darkness, but it is only for a night. It must indeed be a full night, but that is all. Afterwards you will find that everything is given back to you in glorious resurrection; and nothing can measure the difference between what was before and what now is![417]

You might wish to, but you cannot crucify yourself. I was sent a newspaper cutting (from the USA if I remember correctly), which reported police being called to a house where a man had tried to crucify himself on a wooden cross. He had hammered a nail through his feet, and then had hammered a nail through his left hand. Then to his dismay he realized that he could not hammer the last nail into his right hand with only his right hand free! Fortunately he had his mobile phone in his trouser pockets and called for help. But the Lord can crucify you so that you can experience His resurrection life. The apostle Paul declared,

I have been crucified with Christ and I no longer live, but Christ lives in me. The life I now live in the body, I live by faith in the Son of God, who loved me and gave Himself for me. Galatians 2:20

For the first six months after I was born again I was radically on fire for Jesus. Ready to serve Him with all my heart and soul. I was not only successful in business but also determined in the many adventure sports I was engaged in, so imagined I was ready for my call.

Then (in brief) I was thrown into a year of hell. I was relentlessly tormented in my mind both day and night. No words of mine can describe the horror of the situation. Various church leaders did their best to help, but to no avail. I tried the doctor but he could not help either. I was in such constant distress that even friends could not handle my tormented state. Only two lasted the distance. Eventually the wear–and–tear meant I could no longer go to work every day.

Then I had to leave my family home and go and stay with my mother for a while. Month after month after month went by with no respite. God had left me (as I thought from the apparent evidence) and the devil seemed to have full rein in my life. I was broken. Deeply broken. All former props in my life fell down. All prayers seemed to go unanswered. Then on December 27th 1992 at 6:10 pm, it all ended as suddenly as it started.

And then my call came, and the rest is, well, history. The person who emerged was so different to the person who went into that dark night. I know, really, really know, that anything God has done or may do through me is Him entirely.

Welsh–born English poet, orator and Anglican priest George Herbert in his own book of proverbs wrote[418] *God's Mill Grinds Slow, But Sure* and like myself, many of God's saints can say 'amen' to that!

> How should you behave when you might find yourself 'going through hell'? Just keep going!

How do you know when it is the dark night of the soul that you are going through? My best answer? You don't! At least not until it's over and you are aware of the deep work God has done within you.

How should you behave when you might find yourself 'going through hell'? Do what Joyce Meyer recommends: "Just keep going!" I might put it this way: "No matter how dark, how lonely, how isolated, how downcast you feel, do the right thing."

Jesus never asks us to go where He has not. I'll finish this chapter focused on how His ministry began after He had been baptised in the River Jordan.[419]

> *Then Jesus, **being filled with the Holy Spirit**, returned from the Jordan and was led by the Spirit into the wilderness, being tempted for forty days by the devil... Then Jesus returned **in the power of the Spirit** to Galilee, and news of Him went out through all the surrounding region. And He taught in their synagogues, being glorified by all.* Luke 4:1–2 & 14–15 NKJV [emphasis mine]

Some probing questions:

- Can you see what the dark night of the soul might achieve?

- Have you experienced a time in your Christian life that could be described as 'the dark night of the soul?'

THIRTEEN
A Forgotten Truth?

I was born and bred in Belfast. The city is well known for many things, but probably best known for a great ship we built just over a century ago. The *Titanic*. Yes, it sank on its maiden voyage, but it was fine when it left Belfast! Several major films have been made about the ship's demise (including a 1943 version made by Nazi Germany!) The story holds an unfading fascination. The ship 'that even God could not sink',[420] was sunk by a lump of frozen water on a perfectly calm night. We are all intrigued by the individual stories of courage and cowardice that manifested in the rich and the poor aboard that maiden journey. Let me tell you one story you may not have heard.

John Harper was a Scotsman, born 1872, into a Christian family. Saved at the age of 13, he began preaching on the streets as a teenager, so it was no surprise that he became Pastor of Paisley Road Baptist Church at the tender age of 25. The church quickly grew from 25 people to 500 within ten years. He travelled as a preacher all around the British Isles including the Belfast shipyard.

> Saving souls was more pressing in bygone days because there was an understanding that hell was a real place for the unredeemed.

John's reputation as a passionate soul winner reached across the ocean and he was invited to preach at the Chicago church of D.L. Moody. A year later he was invited back again, and this time he purchased *Titanic* tickets for himself, his 6–year–old daughter Nana, and his niece, Jessie. (His wife had died shortly after the birth of their daughter.) On the night of April 14th, 1912, the ship began to founder after hitting the iceberg and, after seeing his daughter safely onboard a lifeboat, he gave up his place on Lifeboat 11. It was reported he was calling out, "Women, children and unsaved into the lifeboats." More than 1500 souls went into the icy water that night, and John Harper was seen swimming to folks asking them if they were saved, even giving away his lifejacket telling the unsaved receiver, "You have greater need of this than me." At a meeting at Hamilton, Canada, in 1916, a Scotsman stood up and told of his life–changing encounter with fellow Scotsman John Harper.

> "I am a survivor of the *Titanic*. When I was drifting along on a spar that awful night, the tide brought Mr. John Harper of Glasgow, also on a piece of wreck near me. "Man", he said, "are you saved?" "No", I said, "I am not." He replied, "Believe on the Lord Jesus Christ and thou shalt be saved," and shortly after he went down; and there alone in the night, and with two miles of water under me, I believed. I am John Harper's last convert."

His story is told in the book, *The Titanic's Last Hero*, published by Moody Adams.

I think that saving souls was more pressing in bygone days because there was an understanding that hell was a real place for the unredeemed.

As a young Christian I served under an amazing minister who, by example, taught me so much about God's love, mercy and grace. One day he called a group of men together and asked us to prepare to be used at a mid–week meeting especially for unsaved men in the neighborhood. He gave us a list of ten questions he might ask us, so that, if called upon to do so, we could be prepared to answer any one of them. When I got home I asked the Lord if there was a question I would be asked, and to my delight, He witnessed to me that I would be asked the question, "What does it mean for you to be born–again?" I was so excited because I knew immediately what I would say. The changes in my life had been truly momentous and I was still in awe of what God had done, and was doing in my life. I could understand why the minister might choose me to answer that question.

Then came the bombshell! The Lord witnessed to me that my natural response was not the one He wished me to give. He wanted me to say I was hell–bound and that being born–again completely changed my eternal destiny. Oh, the pain as I thought what my beloved minister would think of such a response! I had never heard, nor would have expected to hear, the word mentioned in church. The church had grown wonderfully under his ministry based on love, grace and mercy—and these were well seeded into my soul. I was thrown into great indecision. What answer would I give? Would I please man, and in this case such a Godly man, or God?

Then I came to the conclusion I had been mistaken in believing I had heard from God, and a measure of peace returned. Then came the night, and you know what's coming, don't you? The very first question was publicly addressed to me. *"Ken, would you stand up and tell everyone what it means for you to be born–again?"* Shock. Panic. Silence. I stared at the floor. Then I looked up. The minister was smiling, and waiting. Decision time. After what seemed like an eternity, and with head bowed, I began by saying, *"I was hell–bound*

> We are all comfortable with the concept of divine justice but uncomfortable with the concept of hell.

and being born–again completely changed my eternal destiny…" When I had finished my answer I sat down, head still lowered in embarrassment. I risked a quick glance at my beloved minister's face, and wished I hadn't. This gracious man looked taken aback. I left the minor hall quietly at the end of the evening. I just couldn't face looking into his eyes.

Home again, I knelt down in anguished prayer, opened my Bible at random and my eyes went straight to the words, *"Well done, good and faithful servant."* [421] Within a week the event was behind me and all was well again. I managed to push the event safely into the back of my mind. But, as I wrote this chapter, it came back to my memory as fresh as the day it happened and, looking back, I believe that God had seeded this truth deep into my understanding.

I think we are all comfortable with the concept of divine justice but uncomfortable with the concept of hell. However, like John Harper, grasping its reality will almost certainly change how we behave. It will almost certainly change our priorities and almost certainly change our prayers.

Many years ago I picked up a leaflet titled *How To Pray For Your Loved Ones.* It said that, if we truly believed there was a place of eternal damnation for the unredeemed, then seeing loved ones safely into the Kingdom of God would be *the* most important thing in our lives. As such, we should be willing to pray, *"Lord, whatever it takes…"*

I had to ponder this for a while because my prayers for unsaved loved ones leaned more towards asking for God's blessings upon their lives than, *"Lord, whatever it takes…"* I realized I had to decide once and for all what I really believed. That leaflet changed my prayers. And not just for my loved ones.

The Old and New Testament use a variety of different words for *death* and the *grave,* [422] and there are many contrary views on what these words mean. So I needed to check this out for myself and read what Jesus said on this issue. Contrary to some declarations, Jesus spoke of heaven more than hell, but He did speak of hell more than any other Biblical figure.

Approximately 13% of His teaching and about 50% of His parables were about punishment, judgment and hell. Familiar spirits working through spirit mediums and telling people that their unsaved loved ones are safe and happy on the other side is deception.[423] That's just one reason why Scripture warns us *so* strongly to have nothing to do with mediums and familiar spirits.[424] Scripture affirms that we are destined to die once and, after that, to face judgment.[425]

Knowing that Jesus is 'The Truth' and 'The Word who became flesh,' and that He only said what His Father gave Him to say,[426] it is important to invest a few minutes now to read, *really read*, and absorb

- what He said

- how often He said it

- then decide what He clearly intended us to understand from His words.

As Jesus often said, "Whoever has ears, let him hear."[427] When we get to heaven, it will be too late! [All emphases in the verses below are mine.]

Matthew 5:22

> *But I tell you that anyone who is angry with a brother or sister will be subject to judgment. Again, anyone who says to a brother or sister, 'Raca,' is answerable to the court. And anyone who says, 'You fool!' will be in danger of the fire of* **hell**.

Matthew 5:27–30

> *You have heard that it was said, 'You shall not commit adultery.' But I tell you that anyone who looks at a woman lustfully has already committed adultery with her in his heart. If your right eye causes you to stumble, gouge it out and throw it away. It is better for you to lose one part of your body than for your whole body to be thrown into* **hell**. *And if your right hand causes you to stumble, cut it off and throw it away. It is better for you to lose one part of your body than for your whole body to go into* **hell**.

Matthew 8:11–12

> *I say to you that many will come from the east and the west, and will take their places at the feast with Abraham, Isaac and Jacob in the kingdom of heaven. But the subjects of the kingdom will be **thrown outside, into the darkness, where there will be weeping and gnashing of teeth.***

Matthew 10:28

> *Do not be afraid of those who kill the body but cannot kill the soul. Rather, be afraid of the One who can destroy both soul and body in **hell.***

Matthew 13:41–43

> *The Son of Man will send out His angels, and they will weed out of His kingdom everything that causes sin and all who do evil. They will **throw them into the blazing furnace, where there will be weeping and gnashing of teeth.** Then the righteous will shine like the sun in the kingdom of their Father. **Whoever has ears, let them hear.***

Matthew 22:12–13

> *He asked, "How did you get in here without wedding clothes, friend?" The man was speechless. Then the king told the attendants, "Tie him hand and foot, and **throw him outside, into the darkness, where there will be weeping and gnashing of teeth.**"*

Matthew 23:15 NIV

> *Woe to you, teachers of the law and Pharisees, you hypocrites! You travel over land and sea to win a single convert, and when you have succeeded, you make them twice as much a child of **hell** as you are.*

Matthew 23:33

> *You snakes! You brood of vipers! How will you escape being condemned to **hell**?*

Matthew 25:30 & 41 & 46

> *And throw that worthless servant **outside, into the darkness, where there will be weeping and gnashing of teeth.***
>
> *Then He will say to those on his left, '**Depart from Me, you who are cursed, into the eternal fire prepared for the devil and his angels.'***
>
> *Then they will go away to **eternal punishment**, but the righteous to eternal life.*

Mark 9:42–48

> *If anyone causes one of these little ones—those who believe in Me—to stumble, it would be better for them if a large millstone were hung around their neck and they were thrown into the sea. If your hand causes you to stumble, cut it off. It is better for you to enter life maimed than with two hands to go into **hell**, where the fire never goes out. And if your foot causes you to stumble, cut it off. It is better for you to enter life crippled than to have two feet and be thrown into **hell**. And if your eye causes you to stumble, pluck it out. It is better for you to enter the kingdom of God with one eye than to have two eyes and be thrown into **hell**, where '**the worms that eat them do not die, and the fire is not quenched.'***

Luke 13:24–28

> *Make every effort to enter through the narrow door, because many, I tell you, will try to enter and will not be able to. Once the owner of the house gets up and closes the door, you will stand outside knocking and pleading, "Sir, open the door for us." But he will answer, "I don't know you or where you come from." Then you will say, "We ate and drank with you, and you taught in our streets." But he will reply, "I don't know you or where you come from. Away from me, all you evildoers!" **There will be weeping there, and gnashing of teeth**, when you see Abraham, Isaac and Jacob and all the prophets in the kingdom of God, but you yourselves thrown out.*

Even in the last book of the Bible the risen Jesus—the Lion of Judah—is still speaking on this terrible fate for those whose names are not written in the Book of Life.

Revelation 20:12–15

And I saw the dead, great and small, standing before the throne, and books were opened. Another book was opened, which is the book of life. The dead were judged according to what they had done as recorded in the books. The sea gave up the dead that were in it, and death and Hades gave up the dead that were in them, and each person was judged according to what they had done. Then death and Hades were thrown into the lake of fire. **The lake of fire is the second death. Anyone whose name was not found written in the book of life was thrown into the lake of fire.**

> Jesus came to save us, and hell is clearly what He saved us from.

I think it is difficult to miss what Jesus was *clearly* saying. I wish it were not so, but since Jesus spoke truthfully, passionately and continually on this eternal state, I must take it onboard wholeheartedly. If we knew for certain a terrible tsunami was on its way, wouldn't we want to warn people, and tell them to run to higher ground? That's what Jesus was doing.[428] That's why God's offer of grace is such good news!

I used this illustration in my first book, *Loved Like Never Before* and it is appropriate for this chapter. Wherever the train driver goes is where the passengers are going. The devil's train is hell–bound[429] and so are those onboard, while Jesus' passengers are heaven–bound. The German martyr, Dietrich Bonhoeffer, put it better perhaps when he said, "If you are onboard the wrong train, it is no use running along the corridor in the other direction."

Jesus came to save us,[430] and hell is clearly what He *saved us from*. Safety is dismounting from the devil's train, boarding Jesus' train, and staying aboard! If you are reading this book and are not onboard the Saviour's train, get onboard now, and immediately you will be on higher ground. The ticket is free, but it took the cruel cross and the crucified Messiah to purchase your ticket. The love of God made a way where there was no way. His love pursues us. And pursues us.[431]

God did not send Jesus to condemn us, but to *rescue* us from a fate worse than death.[432] Thus, as Christ's body here on earth, our ministry is not to condemn[433] but to warn,[434] to reveal God's passionate father–heart,[435] and be co–workers with Jesus in reconciling a lost world to Himself.[436] Only those onboard the salvation train can confidently exclaim,

> *"O Death where is your sting? O Hades, where is your victory?"*
> 1 Corinthians 15:55 NKJV

Today there is a strong movement to 'improve God's image' to a critical society. The very mention of God's righteous judgment, coming wrath and the reality of hell, has become almost politically incorrect in church life. This deafening silence on these clear Biblical truths sends an unspoken message to the flock that they may safely ignore this unpleasant subject. Which means ignoring what Jesus continually said on the subject. This silence is seriously affecting doctrine within the Body of Christ because, when the teaching on righteous judgment, coming wrath and the reality of hell is removed, new doctrines rise up to take their place.

A Barna survey (2005–2011 USA sample) showed that twenty–five percent of born–again Christians said *all people* are eventually saved or accepted by God. Twenty–six percent said a person's religion doesn't matter because *all faiths* teach the same lessons. Forty percent of born–again Christians said they believe Christians and Muslims worship the *same God*.[437] The implications of these unscriptural beliefs are simply enormous. It would mean that Jesus did not need to send anyone out to all the nations with the gospel after all. Thus, the missionaries who sacrificed *so much* in centuries past to answer that clear command need not have done so! And the millions of men and women who, over the past two thousand years, chose jail, torture or death rather than convert to another faith could have safely converted because all faiths would lead to the same God, and all will be saved!

This ungodly silence on the subject also affects our culture, as people live with no sense they will ever be held to account for their earthly behavior.[438] They don't believe there is anything to be saved from. Theologian and author R.C. Sproul said, "If God is not a God of judgment, if there's no such thing as hell, what good is the Gospel? The Gospel tells us that we're saved from the wrath that is to come."[439]

I'll close this chapter with a piece from the *The Christian Beacon*:[440]

> On an American troopship, the soldiers crowded around their chaplain asking, "Do you believe in hell?" "I do not." "Well, then, will you please resign, for if there is no hell we do not need you, and if there is a hell, we do not wish to be led astray."

Enough said, I hope.

Some probing questions:

- Do you believe that we are all eternal beings?

- Do you believe that 'hell' is as real as Jesus describes?

- *If so*, might that affect whom you pray for, how passionately you pray for them, and how often you pray for them?

- Which of these two sentences is correct? For God so hated the world that He gave His one and only Son, *or*, For God so loved the world that He gave His one and only Son.

FOURTEEN
A Forgotten Word?

Hand in hand with a forgotten truth is a forgotten word. *Sin*. They are inseparable. As the world sinks deeper and deeper into a sin–driven, hell–bound darkness, we seem to be speaking less and less about it. (With some wonderful exceptions, of course.) I heard one preacher say that God is too big to be bothered with our sins.

One might wonder how this view is possible since it was sin that sent Jesus to the cross on our behalf. Moreover, the word 'sin' in all its variations (sin, sins, sinner, sinners, sinned) is mentioned in 245 verses in 21 (out of 27) of the New Testament books. The current mood of the culture makes sin an unwanted, unacceptable topic. An offence. Here's why we need to put the word 'sin' back on the table.

Sin kills *everything* good. It takes no prisoners. It just kills everything. It kills trust. It kills relationships. It kills marriages. It brings nations into deep moral darkness. It starts arguments. It starts violence. It starts wars. It brings anger, malice, hatred and bitterness. It empties purses and fills jails. It promises pleasure but brings pain. Sometimes immediately. Sometimes later. Sometimes a generation away. It addicts people to alcohol, drugs, sex and gambling. It brings shame and guilt. It produces thieves, liars, occultists, adulterers and perverts. It thrives on pornography, dishonesty and unfaithfulness. It produces broken hearts, broken families, broken

> Sin promises to be
>
> a secret friend but
>
> becomes a cruel master..

homes and broken people. It kills babies in the womb and young men on the streets. It feeds crime. And gangs. It bullies, violates, abuses, dominates, manipulates and controls. The fruit of sin brings fear. Terrible relentless fear to the old, the weak and the vulnerable. And to parents. And to children. It sears consciences. It defiles. It pollutes. It imprisons its captives in darkness and blinds their eyes to the Light. Above all, it separates man from the One who truly loves him. Sin promises to be a secret friend but becomes a cruel master. As flies are attracted to dog's dirt, so unclean spirits are attracted to sin.

Sin originated through Adam's disobedience to God and his submission to the serpent's subtle suggestions. It has thus continued to this day. Obedience brings us safely into submission to the Sovereignty and Lordship of Jesus while sin brings us dangerously into submission to the serpent and his rule.

Can you see why no sin will ever be permitted into Heaven?

Can you see why God—in whose presence the angels shout, "Holy Holy Holy"—can have no compromise with it?

Can you see why the devil loves it? It grieves the heart of God[441] because it destroys those made in God's image.[442] It grieves, and even quenches the Spirit of God in a man or woman. Never, ever make friends with sin.

Jesus came to save us from our sins.[443] The cross stands in defiance of sin's relentless, worldwide onslaught. It shouts: "Forgiveness!" It shouts: "Freedom!" It stands as a table prepared for us in the midst of the cruelest of enemies.[444] With an invitation banner over the table saying LOVE.[445] The cross demands our response. Not a luke-warm response. *Sin laughs at such.* The cross

> Moving on with God
>
> means we must see sin
>
> the way God sees it.

demands a turn–around and a bowing of the knee to the One who came to our rescue. It asks for a sin–rejecting, Christ–centered, Blood–cleansed, Spirit–filled life of obedience to the One who leads us safely on paths of righteousness. For His Name's sake.[446] Moving on with God means we must see sin the way God sees it.

A probing question:

• What damage have you seen sin do?

FIFTEEN
The Lines in the Sand

"Go therefore…" Matthew 28:19a NKJV

To move on with God, I think there comes a time when we must move out with God. I pray that the challenges of the earlier chapters have ploughed good soil and sown good seed in preparation for this. But more about this later in the chapter.

First, let me give you my understanding of the days ahead. The days we have been born for. There are many who believe a great end time revival will come and sweep all before it, and then we, as Christians, will be greatly valued again. So far the many, indeed the great many, prophesied dates for this end time revival have come and gone while the world has continued to grow spiritually and morally darker and darker.

We long for the power Christians displayed in the Book of Acts, but forget it happened in the midst of terrible persecution.[447] I believe the events recorded for us by Luke in the Book of Acts are a blueprint for the days that lie ahead. As persecution rises, I am certain we will see the power of God rise.[448] Jesus said He will build His church and the gates of Hades[449] will not prevail,[450] and as the Biblical clock runs down the devil will certainly increase his attempts to prevail.[451] He knows the fate that awaits him.[452] Thus I think we can, and should, expect great things from God in

> Where Christians suffer persecution the church is united and strong, and where the Christians are relatively comfortable, the church is divided and weak.

the coming days, but in the midst of persecution.

Why do I sound this alarm? Because we dress for the weather we expect. Expect pleasant weather and you dress appropriately. Expect storms and you dress accordingly. Expect war and you dress for battle. I don't think that we, in the western nations, are dressed appropriately for what lies ahead. Not so where the church is severely persecuted. It is estimated approximately 150,000 Christians are killed for their faith each year, and this persecution takes place in 130 countries, or roughly two–thirds of all nations on the globe.[453]

Where Christians suffer persecution the church is united and strong, and where the Christians are relatively comfortable, the church is divided and weak. For us, the comfortable ones, that is rapidly changing. In the coming days we will have to face many challenging lines in the sand. On one controversial issue after another we will find ourselves bending and bending, trying to be at peace with all men, until the point comes where we say, "Thus far and no further." And right there is the line in the sand. The line we will not cross.

Young Joseph would not cross the line and commit sexual immorality when Potiphar's wife constantly tried to seduce him.[454] He ended up in jail. Under severe pressure Daniel would not obey the order to worship the King as a god, and was thrown to the lions.[455] Shadrach, Meshach and Abednego would not bow the knee to worship an image set up by the King, and were thrown into the furnace.[456] We know that in these cases God stepped in and rescued them, but this is not always the case— as church history, both ancient and modern, clearly shows. How do we overcome the relentless accuser of the brethren?

They triumphed over him by the blood of the Lamb and by the word of their testimony; they did not love their lives so much as to shrink from death. Revelation 12:11

There are, however, lines in the sand that we should cross over, but the perceived cost of crossing them can make many of us turn back. The 'church in the wilderness' under Moses was destined for the fruit–filled Promised Land called Canaan,[457] but at Kadesh Barnea they reached their line in the sand, their moment of decision, and turned back. They saw the landscape where they were being called to live was occupied by men of considerable stature.[458] These 'giants' striding across it saw God's people as grasshoppers, and sadly God's people saw themselves as grasshoppers.[459]

Only two men, Joshua and Caleb, saw Canaan through God's eyes and knew they could take their inheritance.[460] Scripture says these two men followed the Lord wholeheartedly.[461] The rest of the congregation was too fearful to move on with God any further. This detailed journey of the church in the wilderness is a natural picture, or mirror image of the spiritual.[462] Natural Canaan was their fruit–filled destiny and 'spiritual Canaan' is ours.[463] Kevin Conner's book Interpreting the Symbols and Types says that Canaan stands for 'the believer's inheritance gained by warfare'.[464] Thus we may settle it now that our spiritual fruit–bearing inheritance will always be contested! (Sadly Canaan is often and only linked to heaven, but I assure you that, if you get to heaven and there are giants to fight, you are in the wrong place!) I have come to believe that the believer's spiritual land of promise is discipleship. Fruit and discipleship are inseparable.

This is to My Father's glory, that you bear much fruit, showing yourselves to be My disciples. John 15:8

Today, and in increasing numbers, aggressive anti–Christian men of considerable stature stride across our landscape, and in their eyes, and so often in our own eyes, we seem like grasshoppers. Jesus of course, sees things differently, and invites us, as believers, to cross that unseen line in the sand and enter into the fullness of our destiny as His disciples. First though, He asks us to count the cost so that, if we put our hand

> The true church is wonderfully awash with believers, but in truth, few are disciples.

to the plow, we won't look back.[465] So that if we start, we won't give up. Wholehearted following works! Lukewarm doesn't.

*Whoever wants to be My disciple must deny themselves and take up their cross and follow Me. For whoever wants to save their life will lose it, **but whoever loses their life for Me will find it.***

Matthew 16: 24–25 [emphasis mine]

*If anyone comes to Me and does not hate father and mother, wife and children, brothers and sisters—**yes, even their own life**—such a person cannot be My disciple. And whoever does not **carry their cross** and follow Me cannot be My disciple. Suppose one of you wants to build a tower. Won't **you first sit down and estimate the cost** to see if you have enough money to complete it? For if you lay the foundation and are not able to finish it, everyone who sees it will ridicule you, saying, "This person began to build and **wasn't able to finish.**" Or suppose a king is about to go to war against another king. Won't he first sit down and consider whether he is able with ten thousand men to oppose the one coming against him with twenty thousand? If he is not able, he will send a delegation while the other is still a long way off and will ask for terms of peace. **In the same way, those of you who do not give up everything you have cannot be My disciples.***[466]
Luke 14:26–33 [emphasis mine]

There it is then! The line in the sand that we, as believers, are invited to cross. The true church is wonderfully awash with believers, but in truth, few are disciples. Yet Jesus sent the first disciples out to replicate themselves.[467] Is the call going forth?

So what does moving out have to do with moving on? As always, Jesus is the best example. He taught in the temple courts every day when He was in Jerusalem,[468] but spent much more time out and about in rural Galilee. Those in and around the temple would probably have developed temple–centered lives and a temple–centered language, and I suspect that 'outsiders' would have viewed its spiritual culture as somewhat strange and intimidating. Jesus didn't wait for these outsiders to come to the temple courts to meet Him and hear the good news. Instead, He went out amongst them and met them where they were. The rough fishermen by the sea of Galilee.[469] The Samaritan woman at the well.[470] The hated tax collectors.[471] Along the way, because of His close interaction with the 'un–churched' people, the Pharisees and their liberal counterparts, the Sadducees, accused Him of being a glutton and a drunkard, a friend of tax collectors and sinners,[472] the people least likely to be heading to the temple or any of the estimated four hundred and eighty synagogues in the city.[473] Out amongst the people, Jesus encountered the sick,[474] the demonized,[475] the untouchables[476] and the outcasts.[477] He had compassion for them all, and they loved Him.[478] This was the Kingdom work that He modeled for His disciples, and the work that He trained them for.[479] He never tried to glamorize the calling, but warned them that, in commissioning them for this work, He was sending them out like sheep amongst wolves.[480]

> As His fellow workers, will we follow Jesus out into the community, where the fields are white unto harvest, but the laborers few?

Today, as His fellow workers,[481] will we follow Jesus out into the community, where the fields are white unto harvest,[482] but the laborers few?[483] Will we allow Him, by His Spirit working through us, to love the unlovable, to save those, whom to us, seem un–saveable, to comfort the discomforted, and at times, discomfort the comfortable in their sins?[484] To feel the joy of service to the King,[485] knowing that our labour for Him is not in vain.[486] To bear fruit.[487] To sometimes suffer rejection, insults and disappointments.[488]

Isn't that a challenge? An adventure? A privilege. An honour.

> The fragrance of Christ
>
> upon your life
>
> will be the aroma
>
> of life to some,
>
> but to others, not so.

Or, will we always live in and around the safety and security of 'the temple' and wait for the lonely, the hurting, the grieving and the rest to come looking for us?

Finally, some words of caution. Don't be a lone sheep amongst wolves! Jesus was able to move amongst the 'unsaved' and be in their 'ungodly' midst because He was the strongest one there. Always be part of a team. Jesus sent disciples out in pairs. Too often, immature Christians have enthusiastically moved out of the shelter of church life too early, alone and unsupervised, and found themselves quickly overwhelmed. One man I know, a recent convert, went with his unsaved friends to the pub in order to be a Christian witness in their midst, but sadly, once in that familiar environment he quickly fell back into his old ways. He was still a baby Christian. Today he is stronger.

Most established ministries have good training programmes and provide spiritual cover and accountability. Remember that 'good ideas' might not be 'God ideas', so it's worth waiting on God for His leading. The skilful fishermen worked all night and caught nothing. One directional sentence from Jesus and their nets were full![489] That story is there for a reason. Remember too, that God watches over His word.[490] Not the world's word or a mixture of the two.

The fragrance of Christ upon your life will be the aroma of life to some, but to others, not so.[491] If someone wants to argue with you, try to discern if they want to argue in a genuine attempt to find truth, or merely to mock your beliefs. You carry precious pearls.[492] Cast them carefully. Plan for the long haul, and don't set a pace that will burn you out or take down your family life! Don't be frightened to build in ample rest periods.[493] I learnt this the hard way early on! Develop perseverance and patience.[494] Value encouragers; they are priceless! And be an encourager to others.[495]

It is good practice to number your days, to value them, and invest wisely in them. Each one is a precious gift from God. One day we will cross that final line in the sand, and what a homecoming that will be. We will finally see His face![496] Let us plan to cross that line in celebration and triumph!

Meanwhile, let the adventure begin!

"...and lo, I am with you always, even to the end of the age." Matthew 28:20b NKJV

Notes

1. Philippians 1:13

Introduction

2. 'lite' - a computer term meaning a scaled down version of the full program, and a term used for reduced calorie foods like milk or margarine

3. If you don't know you are loved, please start with my first book, *Loved Like Never Before*. ISBN: 978-1852405854

4. Matthew 9:9

Chapter 1

5. Genesis 2:16-17

6. Genesis 3:4-7

7. Song of songs 2:4

8. 1891, Sermon #2209

9. *'Jesus, all for Jesus'* by Robin Mark

10. Luke 19:14

11. Romans 6:17

12. Mark 4:41

13. Luke 5:4-7

14. Luke 10:17

15. Charles Spurgeon, *The Soul Winner*, Christian Focus Publications, 1992, 24-25, 26

16. Luke 11:4

17. Luke 6:46 Matthew 7:21

18. Mark 10:15

19. Revelation chapters 2 & 3

20. Romans 6:15-17

21. Ephesians 5:25

22. Romans 8:15-16

23. 1 Timothy 5:17

24. Romans 13:1-7

25. James 4:4

26. Revelation 3:20

Chapter 2

27. Romans 5:6

28. John 3:16

29. Hebrews 7:27 & 9:12

30. John 19:30

31. Philippians 1:11 Titus 3:6 Hebrews 13:21

32. John 10:11 1 Corinthians 13:1-13

33. Matthew 28:19-20
34. Romans 12:1
35. 2 Corinthians 5:14-15
36. Matthew 16:24-25
37. Deuteronomy 15:21
38. Exodus 29:36
39. 1 Corinthians 11:1
40. 2 Corinthians 4:17
41. Psalm 95:2 & 100:4
42. John 4:23-24
43. James 2:14-26
44. Deuteronomy 15:21
45. Hebrews 4:15 1 Peter 1:19
46. Matthew 6:21
47. 2 Corinthians 5:14-15
48. Loved Like Never Before. ISBN: 978-1852405854
49. Malachi 3:10
50. Acts 10:4 NKJV
51. 1 Kings 7:42
52. 1 Corinthians 3:8-9

Chapter 3
53. http://www.youtube.com/watch?v=TyBKz1wdK0M
54. John 12:31 John 14:30 John 16:11
55. Ephesians 2:2
56. 2 Corinthians 4:4
57. Colossians 1:13
58. 1 John 5:19
59. Genesis 1:26
60. Romans 2:14-15
61. Isaiah 30:21
62. Deuteronomy 30:19
63. John 10:10
64. 2 Corinthians 3:17
65. Genesis 3:1-4
66. 1 John 5:19
67. 2 Corinthians 11:3 & Revelation 20:10
68. http://news.bbc.co.uk/1/hi/programmes/breakfast/4152041.stm
69. http://www.bbc.co.uk/complaints/pdf/apps_springer.pdf
70. http://www.guardian.co.uk/uk/2002/nov/21/britishidentity.features11
71. http://en.wikipedia.org/wiki/Let's_Spend_the_Night_Together
72. http://internet-filter-review.toptenreviews.com/internet-pornography-statistics.html

73. Daily Mail Monday April 3rd 2012, p14 The Melanie Phillips column
74. http://www.bbc.co.uk/news/10498595
75. http://www.telegraph.co.uk/news/politics/1950333/Women-should-have-abortion-on-demand.html
76. *When Fables Fall*. Arthur Francis Green, Sovereign World; p107
77. UK Office for national statistics.
78. http://www.guardian.co.uk/society/2013/jul/15/liverpool-care-pathway-independent-review
79. http://www.dailymail.co.uk/news/article-2161869/Top-doctors-chilling-claim-The-NHS-kills-130-000-elderly-patients-year.html
80. http://www.bbc.co.uk/news/uk-11923107
81. http://www.guardian.co.uk/society/2012/oct/21/puberty-adolescence-childhood-onset
82. Alan Guttmacher Institute. *Sex and America's Teenagers*. New York, NY: Alan Guttmacher Institute, 1994
83. http://www.telegraph.co.uk/health/healthnews/9070891/Dramatic-rise-in-teenage-girls-seeking-contraceptive-implants.html
84. http://www.christian.org.uk/news/age-of-consent-protects-kids-against-heartbreak/
85. http://www.telegraph.co.uk/news/uknews/1542843/Drop-age-of-consent-to-14-says-academic.html
86. http://b4uact.org
87. http://www.ipce.info/newsletters/e_14/gie_ethics.htm
88. http://www.greeleygazette.com/press/?p=11517
89. http://news.bbc.co.uk/1/hi/world/europe/5187010.stm
90. http://www. http://creation.com/slippery-slope
91. James 4:4
92. http://www.graceonlinelibrary.org/church-ministry/pastoral-ministry/sexual-immorality-church-leaders/
93. Nehemiah 2:13
94. From a John Bevere quote
95. Matthew 5:13-14
96. Acts 1:8 2 Corinthians 3:3 2 Corinthians 5:20
97. Matthew 5:14 John 8:12 Isaiah 60:1-2
98. Ephesians 1:4
99. Philippians 2:12 2 Corinthians 7:1
100. 1 Peter 2:9
101. 2 Corinthians 6:14-18
102. Amos 3:3
103. Proverbs 3:6

Chapter 4
104. 2 Corinthians 4:4
105. Romans 5:8
106. 2 Corinthians 6:18

107. Romans 8:16
108. John 8:7-11
109. 1 Corinthians 13:8
110. Mark 16:15
111. 2 Peter 3:9
112. Matthew 25:40
113. Mark 12:31
114. Luke 10:30-38
115. John 4:9
116. Matthew 9:37

Chapter 5
117. Matthew 5:14-16
118. Matthew 28:19
119. 2 Kings 17:36 Psalm 106:8 Acts 13:17 Ephesians 6:10
120. Romans 10:9-10
121. Numbers 11:17 Judges 14:6 Acts 1:8 Romans 15:19
122. Romans 10:17
123. Isaiah 14:12
124. Matthew 4:1
125. Psalm 89:8
126. Luke 2:14
127. Matthew 6:30 & 8:26 & 14:31 & 16:8 & 17:20
128. Genesis 3:1
129. Matthew 4:3
130. Revelation 2:4
131. Revelation 3:16
132. Revelation 21:27
133. Isaiah 60:1-3
134. Jeremiah 29:11
135. Psalm 91
136. Psalm 119:105
137. Psalm 119:11
138. Romans 12:1-2
139. Psalm 66:18

Chapter 6
140. Examples: Infant or believer baptism? Gifts of the Spirit, historical or continuous?
141. Matthew 1:23
142. John 1:14
143. John 14:6
144. John 1:1
145. John 8:45
146. 1 Corinthians 1 19-21

147. http://www.icr.org/article/164/

148. http://www.icr.org/article/does-scripture-allow-gap/

149. http://creation.com/soft-gap-sophistryhttp://www.icr.org/article/does-scripture-allow-gap/

150. http://www.answersingenesis.org/articles/2011/06/21/framework-hypothesis

151. http://creation.com/why-i-rejected-theistic-evolution

152. http://www.answersingenesis.org/articles/1997/12/29/days-revelation-creation

153. http://www.icr.org/article/121/

154. http://creation.com/pre-adamic-man-were-there-human-beings-on-earth-before-adam

155. http://www.answersingenesis.org/articles/nab/gap-ruin-reconstruction-theories

156. http://www.answersingenesis.org/articles/am/v2/n1/mind-the-gap

157. Genesis 2:17

158. Matthew 19:4 Mark 10:5-6

159. Luke, Romans, 1 Corinthians, 1 Timothy, Jude

160. http://www.albertmohler.com/2011/08/31/adam-and-eve-clarifying-again-what-is-at-stake/

161. Frank Zindler, American atheist, in a debate with William Craig, *Atheism vs Christianity* video, Zondervan, 1996

162. G. Richard Bogart, 'The Meaning of Evolution', *American Atheist*, p. 30. 20 September 1979

163. *Loved Like Never Before*, chapter four, 'Seeing the Father's Heart'

164. Creation.com, Answers in Genesis Institute of Creation research

165. Example: '*The Greatest Hoax on Earth? Refuting Dawkins on evolution.*' J. Sarfati

166. http://bible.org/seriespage/overview-book-genesis

167. Genesis 7:18-20

168. Hebrews 13:8

169. 2 Peter 2:5-6

170. Revelation 12:9 & 20:2

171. Matthew 4:10 Mark 7:10 Luke 18:20 John 7:23

172. John 1:14

173. 2 peter 1:20-21

174. 1 Timothy 3:16

175. *Uproar in the Church*. ISBN 901144003 DPM-UK page 15

176. Luke 16:22-28 Matthew 13:40-42 Matthew 25:41 Revelation 20:15

177. http://www.albertmohler.com/2010/05/12/all-roads-lead-to-heaven-kathleen-parker-does-theology/

178. John 14:6

179. John 14:6

180. 1 Corinthians 2:14

181. Brian Edwards '*Nothing but the truth*'. Evangelical Press; p.334

182. http://news.bbc.co.uk/1/hi/uk/393479.stm

183. 1 Corinthians 15:22

184. http://www.barna.org/barna-update/article/21-transformation/252-barna-survey-examines-changes-in-worldview-among-christians-over-the-past-13-years
185. James 3:1
186. Psalm 133
187. Genesis 3:1
188. Ephesians 6:17
189. Matthew 4:4 & 6 & 10
190. Judges 16:19-21

Chapter 7

191. Ephesians 6:14
192. Matthew 4:4,6,10
193. Ephesians 6:17
194. Ephesians 6:10-17
195. Matthew 12:26 & 28
196. Matthew 10:1
197. 2 Corinthians 6:7 & 10:4
198. 1 Peter 5:8
199. John 8:32
200. 2 Corinthians 11: 3-4
201. Jeremiah 1:12
202. James 1:22 1 John 2:5
203. Genesis 3:1
204. Revelation 12:9 & 13:14
205. Matthew 4:1
206. Zechariah 3:1
207. 2 Corinthians 12:7
208. Luke 4:3
209. 1 Corinthians 6:9-12
210. Spurgeon's Morning & Evening January 25th evening
211. Colossians 1:13
212. Romans 12:17-18 1 Corinthians 10:12 Ephesians 5:15
213. 1 Corinthians 11:28
214. The central theme in Jesus' message to the churches in Revelation 2 & 3
215. Ephesians 5:18b
216. Ephesians 4:30
217. 1 Thessalonians 5:19
218. Song of songs 2:15
219. John 10:10
220. Isaiah 5:4-6 Judges 3:7-8
221. Joshua 7
222. Psalm 51
223. John 19:30 Psalm 103:11-12

Chapter 8

224. 2 Chronicles 6:18
225. Exodus 26:13
226. Leviticus 16 Hebrews 9:7
227. Hebrews 9:6-8
228. 1 Kings 6:7
229. 1 Kings 6:18
230. 1 Kings 6:22
231. 1 Kings chapter 8
232. Mark 15:38
233. Acts 7:47-50 Acts 17: 24
234. Hebrews 9:11
235. 2 Corinthians 1:20
236. Hebrews 9:11–14 & 24-26
237. Romans 6:11
238. 2 Corinthians 5:18
239. John 2:19-22
240. Colossians 2:9
241. Romans 12:5 & 16:3
242. Romans 8:9
243. Ephesians 2:22
244. John 14:21 Ephesians 6:24
245. Ephesians 1:4 2 Timothy 1:9
246. Luke 11:36
247. 1 Timothy 5:17

Chapter 9

248. Luke 15:11-32
249. Isaiah 61:10
250. Luke 15:10
251. Philippians 4:3 Revelation 3:5
252. Romans 8:17
253. Colossians 3:7-9
254. For instance, Ellel Ministries International has centers throughout the world.
255. Matthew 15:22-28
256. http://news.google.com/newspapers?nid=2507&dat=19890802&id=RGFAAAA AIBAJ&sjid=MFkMAAAAIBAJ&pg=6713,444792
257. The instructor was found guilty, then on appeal the verdict was quashed and he sued the media who had branded him a bully
258. Matthew 1:23
259. Hebrews 13:20
260. Matthew 10: 1 & 7-9
261. Matthew 15:25-28

262. Matthew 28:19-20
263. Luke 18:27
Chapter 10
264. Exodus 13:21
265. Matthew 4:19
266. John 10:14
267. Jeremiah 29:11
268. Luke 14:25-33
269. Psalm 23:3
270. Isaiah 35:8
271. Chapter one
272. Proverbs 3:6
273. Psalm 119:105
274. Mark 4:23 Revelation 2:7
275. John 12:31 John 14:30 John 16:11
276. 2 Corinthians 6:1
277. Mark 16:17 Luke 4:18 Acts 10:45-47
278. Psalm 51:10 & 17 Psalm 73:21 Psalm 77:6 Psalm 143:4
279. Deuteronomy 4:29 6:5 10:12 11:13 26:16 30:2
280. Deuteronomy 6:5 2 Kings 23:25 Psalm 84:2 Mark 12:30
281. Mark 6:52 Hebrews 3:7
282. Hebrews 3:13
283. Proverbs 17:20
284. Hosea 10:2
285. Proverbs 4:23 Philippians 4:7
286. 2 Timothy 2:22
287. 2 Chronicles 34:27
288. Ephesians 4:31
289. 1 Kings 8:61 Luke 10:27
290. Acts 2:4
291. 1 Corinthians 13:12 KJV
292. 1 Timothy 4:2
293. John 4:24
294. Numbers 22:28
295. Daniel 5:5
296. 1 Corinthians 13:12
297. Colossians 3:15
298. John 14:27 Romans 15:23
299. Genesis 3:8-19
300. Exodus 4:10
301. 1 Corinthians 10:1-6 & 15:46
302. Psalm 23:2

303. 1 Corinthians 6:17
304. Mark 12:30
305. 2 Corinthians 4:4
306. Romans 1:9
307. Acts 2:37
308. Jeremiah 18:1-6
309. Matthew 2:9
310. Acts 2:17
311. 1 Kings 3:5
312. Acts 16:9 perhaps
313. Jude 6
314. Colossians 1:13
315. John 8:12
316. Psalm 91:9-11 Luke 4:1-13 Acts 5:1-3
317. Genesis chapter 3
318. 1 John 1:7 & 2:10
319. 1 Corinthians 3:19
320. Ephesians 1:17 2 peter 3:15
321. 1 Kings 3:5
322. 1 Kings 3:10
323. 1 Corinthians 2:16
324. Matthew 9:4 12:25
325. John 7:7 12:31 15:18-19
326. Matthew 15:19 Romans 8:5-8
327. Ephesians 2:2
328. Romans 6:16
329. James 4:4-5
330. Romans 12:2 Ephesians 4:23
331. http://www.focusonthefamily.com/faith/christian_worldview/whats_a_christian_worldview.aspx
332. Chapter 2: How to boil a frog
333. 2 Corinthians 10:5
334. 2 Timothy 1:7
335. Romans 8:16 1 Corinthians 2:11 Galatians 6:18
336. 1 Corinthians 6:17
337. 1 Chronicles 29:17 2 Chronicles 32:31
338. John 6:51, 54, 55
339. Acts 23:1 2 Corinthians 1:12 1 John 2:6
340. Psalm 42:1
341. See chapter ten in my first book *Loved Like Never Before*
342. Psalm 66:18 1 John 1:8-9
343. Revelation 3:16

344. John 14:23-24
345. Loved like never before. ISBN: 978-1852405854
346. 1 Peter 5:8
347. John 15:1-2
348. ISBN 0-88419-575-9
349. Judges 6:36-40
350. John 10:10
351. Mark 3:9
352. John 7:38

Chapter 11
353. John 1:12
354. Ephesians 4:14
355. 1 Peter 2:2
356. 1 Corinthians 3:2 Hebrews 5:12-13
357. Luke 2:49
358. Deuteronomy 33:1
359. 1 Samuel 9:6
360. 2 Chronicles 8:14
361. Isaiah 61:3b
362. 1 Corinthians 11:1
363. 1 Corinthians 4: 14-16
364. Matthew 26:35 with Luke 22:56-58
365. Hebrews 13:17
366. Ephesians 5:8 & 11
367. John 14:15
368. James chapter 4
369. Genesis 3:8
370. 1 Corinthians 15:45
371. Mark 1:35-38
372. Genesis 2:16-17
373. Genesis 3:4
374. 2 Corinthians 4:4
375. Ephesians 2:1-2 & 5 Colossians 2:13
376. Ephesians 6:12
377. 1 John 5:19
378. Luke 4:5-7 Romans 5:12
379. Ephesians 2:13
380. Colossians 2:13
381. Matthew 6:10
382. Galatians 2:20
383. Mark 14:38
384. Luke 22:42

385. Sparkling Gems Greek word studies. Rick Renner: p 514 Teach All Nations

386. 1 John 3:9 1 Peter 1:23

387. 1 John 3:6

388. Matthew 6:10 &12:28 Luke 22:18

389. 1 Thessalonians 5:23

390. 2 Corinthians 13:11

391. 2 Corinthians 10:5

392. Galatians 5:23-24

393. John 15:1-8

394. Ephesians 2:8

395. 2 Corinthains 2:15

396. Mark 13:13

397. 2 Corinthians 7:1

398. John 8:44

399. Matthew 6:9

400. John 8:12

401. 1 Peter 1:22

402. 3 John 1:2

403. Matthew 18:1-3

404. John 14:23-24

405. Credit; Much of this chapter's understanding came from Tom Marshall's book, *Free Indeed! Fullness for the Whole Man, Spirit, Soul and Body.* ISBN-10: 1852400021

406. Numbers 13:31-33

407. Numbers 14:24

Chapter 12

408. *Abandoned to God*, Oswald Chambers, page 79

409. *Burnout*, Loren Sandford, p. 126

410. Genesis 41:46

411. Genesis 37: 19-36

412. Genesis 41

413. Exodus 2:1-10

414. Exodus 8:1

415. Acts 7:21-22

416. http://www.jewishencyclopedia.com/articles/13766-sinai-mount

417. *The Normal Christian Life*, Watchman Nee, Chapter 13

418. 'Jacula Prudentum', George Herbert. Anglican priest

419. Luke 3:21-22

Chapter 13

420. http://www.archives.gov/exhibits/american_originals/titanic.html

421. Matthew 25:21

422. http://new.bereanbiblesociety.org/hell-sheol-hades-paradise-and-the-grave/

423. Hebrews 9:27

424. Leviticus 19:31 & 20:6 & 20:7
425. Hebrews 9:27
426. John 12:50
427. Matthew 11:15 & 13:9 & 13:43
428. Romans 5:8-9 1 Thessalonians 1:10
429. Revelation 20:10
430. Luke 19:10 John 3:17 John 12:47
431. Romans 5:8-10
432. John 3:16-17
433. John 8:11
434. John 3:36
435. Matthew 18:14 Luke 15:20-24
436. John 1:12 2 Corinthians 5:18-20
437. http://www.christianpost.com/news/many-born-again-christians-hold-universalist-view-barna-finds-49883/#KbbCw87Qo1BxPGYR.99
438. Hebrews 4:13
439. http://www.cbn.com/cbnnews/us/2007/March/Most-Dont-Believe-in-Hell/
440. Published by Collingswood Presbyterian Church. 1936-1976

Chapter 14
441. Genesis 6:6
442. Genesis 1:26
443. Matthew 1:21
444. Psalm 23:5
445. Song of songs 2:4
446. Psalm 23:3

Chapter 15
447. Acts 8:1 Hebrews 10:32
448. Isaiah 60:1-2
449. Hades; god of the underworld
450. Matthew 16:18
451. Revelation 12:12
452. Revelation 20:10
453. http://christianity.about.com/b/2013/01/04/the-silent-story-of-christian-persecution.htm
454. Genesis 39
455. Daniel 6
456. Daniel 3
457. Exodus 13:11 Numbers 13:23-24
458. Numbers 13:28 & 31-32
459. Numbers 13:33
460. Numbers 13:30
461. Deuteronomy 1:35-36

462. 1 Corinthians 10:1-11 & 15:46
463. John 15:16
464. *Interpreting the symbols and types*, Kevin Conner, Temple Publications, page 133
465. Luke 9:62
466. That means Jesus has first call on your life
467. Matthew 28:19-20
468. Matthew 26:55 Luke 19:47
469. Matthew 4:12-25
470. John 4:1-26
471. Luke 5:27 & 19:2-5
472. Matthew 11:19
473. www.jewishvirtuallibrary.org/jsource/History/sadducees_pharisees_essenes.html
474. Matthew 4:23
475. Matthew 8:28-29 &15:22
476. Matthew 8:2
477. Luke 7:37-39 John 8:3-4
478. Matthew 9:36 & 14:14 & 20:34
479. Matthew 10
480. Matthew 10:16
481. 2 Corinthians 6:1
482. John 4:35
483. Matthew 9:37
484. 1 Timothy 1:9-10
485. John 15:10-11
486. 1 Corinthians 15:58
487. John 15:5
488. 2 Corinthians 6:4-10
489. Luke 5:4-6
490. Isaiah 55:11
491. 2 Corinthians 2:16
492. Matthew 7:6
493. Mark 6:31 John 4:6
494. James 5:10-11
495. Acts 11:23 & 16:40 & Acts 18:27
496. Revelation 22:4

About the author

Ken Symington, born 1947, is from Northern Ireland. Although raised in a Christian home, he did not commit his life to Jesus until 1989, at the age of forty–two. In 1994, at the height of a successful business career in advertising, he heard the call of God and left the business world to follow Jesus, wherever that may lead. He founded *Christian Restoration in Ireland*; a ministry involved in teaching, prayer ministry and discipleship training. He has now taught God's Word in nearly twenty nations around the world, and has been an associate teacher with Ellel Ministries International since 1997. His first book, *Loved Like Never Before—Discovering the Father–Heart of God,* has had a profound effect on many lives. Ken has been married to Linda for more than thirty years, and they have three sons, one daughter and four grandchildren. He is a keen landscape photographer.

Lightning Source UK Ltd.
Milton Keynes UK
UKOW06f0800130316

270072UK00001B/7/P